WHILE I CAN

Jo Dibblee

Praise for While I Can

Don't underestimate the importance of the message that *While I Can* conveys. This book will inspire you to step out of your comfort zone to try something entirely different, no matter how difficult it may seem to you at first. Jo shows us that life is worth living in its fullness, which includes caring for those in need. —Nino Lobiladze

One day you might wake up and realize all the plans you have been setting aside for retirement could be missed if you don't seize the day. *While I Can: Finding Purpose and Legacy in a Distant Land* is unreservedly inspirational, heartwarming, and well worth a read if you've ever thought about changing your life. —Melanie Kennedy

I recommend this book for anyone who wants an enjoyable travel adventure story as well as for those who want to be inspired by a tale of courage, risk taking, and ultimately, fulfillment. —Joe Wisinski

Jo Dibblee's profound work, *While I Can*, encourages us to remain curious and live a life of meaning. It motivates us to think about what is most important in life and to spend our time on what really matters. Written with wit and packed with many wise lessons, every reader will gain immensely from reading the book. —Edith Wairimu

While I Can has opened my eyes and taught me that life is mine to live. Jo's book is a meaningful read that simply and succinctly delivers its message to all readers, reminding us to value our time, be humble, and treasure the relationships we have built along the way. This heartwarming, bright tale is not afraid to reveal the ups and downs of life. She taught me many valuable lessons I will never forget. —Jessica Barbosa

WHILE I CAN

Finding Purpose and Legacy in a Distant Land

Jo Dibblee

Team Humanity Baja Press

This memoir is a work of art, and as such, I do not claim it to be purely
objective. Some of my recollections are certainly colored by my perspective.
From the best of my memory, I have shared conversations and significant
moments in my life. This book is not meant to be a how-to guide on living
in Mexico. Rather, it's a sharing of our journey to living our best life.

To all those who are living with challenges,
be they emotional, financial, or physical,
and especially for those living with a terminal illness,
or simply stuck in their own story.

Contents

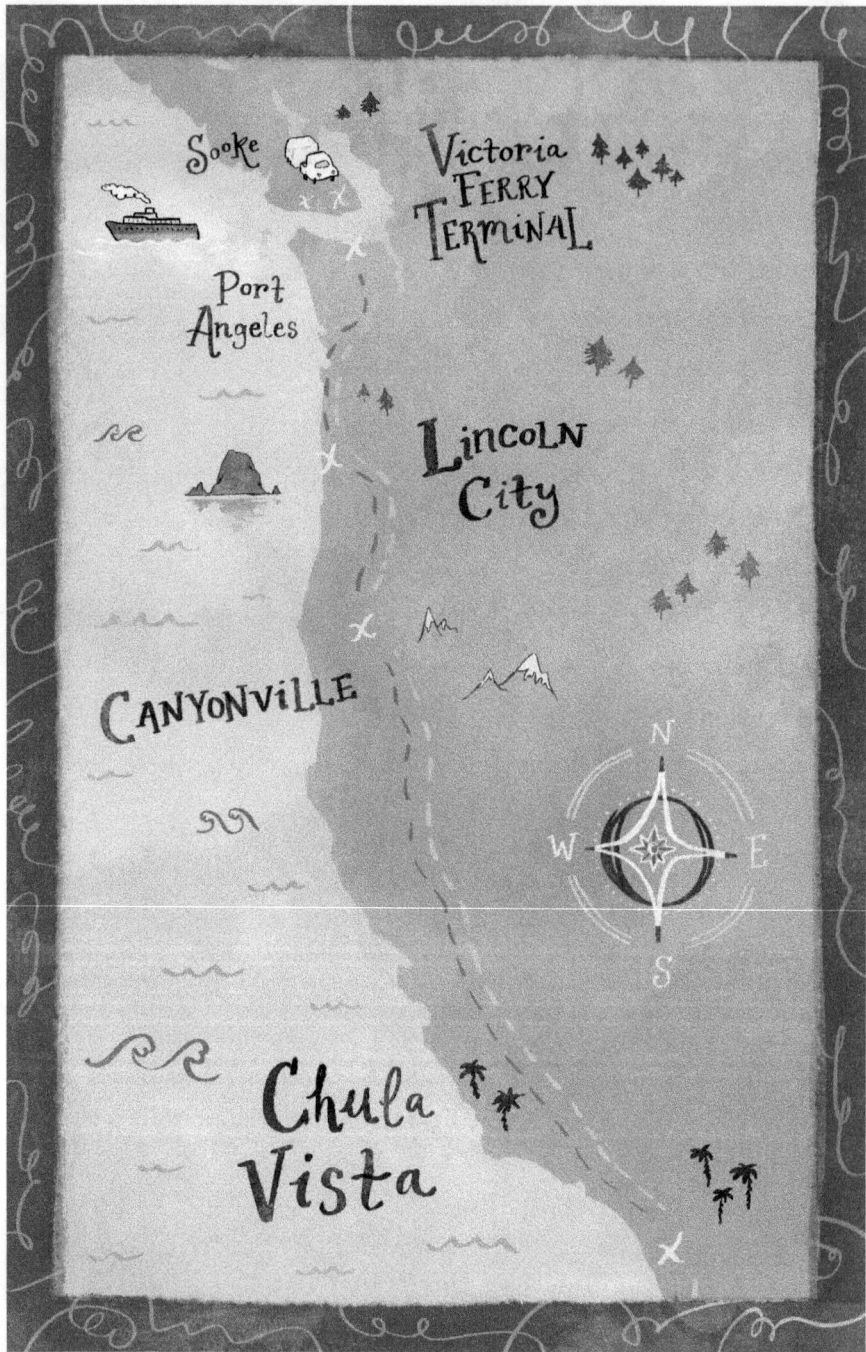

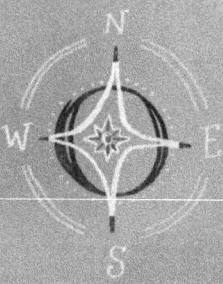

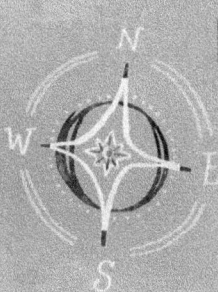

None of us are getting out of here alive,
so please stop treating yourself like an afterthought.
Eat the delicious food. Walk in the sunshine.
Jump in the ocean.
Say the truth that you're carrying in your heart
like hidden treasure.
Be silly. Be kind. Be weird.
There's no time for anything else.

—NANEA HOFFMAN

Sunrise

I stood on the terrace, watching the sun crest the horizon on the Sea of Cortez, listening to the birds sing their morning song with my high-test tea in hand. With the scent of lavender filling the air, I was taken back to the day in Cabo Pulmo when I emerged from the turquoise waters and shouted, "Yes!" Yes, to living the unconventional life, despite what I had been told.

"Stand on your story; not in it," has been my mantra since I began writing nonfiction. Thank goodness, because my story, and maybe yours, is full of reasons not to stand but to stay in the middle of the muck and mire. For some, this means never moving forward and never letting go of the past.

A dear friend once told me, "I'd rather be ailing," as all he focused on was the diagnosis, and not about living his life. His attitude concerned me more than his illness. Our conversations revolved around the next test and impending doom. As he called it, "the check-out date." Meanwhile, life was going on—with or without him. The trouble is, we think we have time, and we do—until we don't.

He appeared to have made a soul agreement to suffer endlessly without hope or reprieve. For years, I watched him succumb more and more to his illness. Sadly, he never felt worthy or truly loved, yet he was one of the kindest and most caring people I have ever known.

The more we lean into an outcome, the more we attract that very outcome. At birth, or perhaps even before, we make a soul agreement on how we will live life; we set our life in motion. From time to time, we are dealt bad hands. When we are, it may seem easier to succumb to the tragedy and stand still in the story, letting the condition or cir-cumstance dictate our life.

A diagnosis of a terminal illness can take anyone down. Rising and standing on that diagnosis in order to live our best life—despite the impending doom—is what creates a legacy and inspires others. Whatever our soul agreement, I believe we can rise to live without apology or regret.

I'm not sure when I discovered my soul agreement. I do know it has been my compass throughout my life. These principles are non-ne-gotiable for me:

» Be a good human; be kind, compassionate, and a light for others.

» Live in gratitude with grace; take nothing for granted.

» Discover your purpose and have the courage to live it; don't settle for less.

» Do meaningful work and serve without expectation; make your life count and live your legacy.

» Stay curious; see life through the eyes of a child.

» Have lots of tea and chocolate in your life, too!

While I Can is written for those who dare to live, who dare to put it all on the line, and who have the courage to live life. I want to inspire you. Are you someone graced with a full, rich life of health, longevity, and prosperity? If so, don't squander it. Instead use up every blessing you have. While I Can is about daring to live courageously, despite what hand has been dealt. Sometimes life sucks—and sometimes its glorious.

This is a story of how a retired firefighter and his entrepreneur wife threw caution to the wind, despite knowing the clock was ticking. We traded the comforts of our spacious, five-bedroom home in Canada on beautiful Vancouver Island for a tiny home on wheels and headed to Baja California Sur, Mexico.

All because it was time. We knew the clock was ticking.

Do you realize the average person in North America retires between the ages of sixty-two and sixty-seven? The average lifespan in the United States is seventy-eight, with Canadians faring only slightly older until age eighty-two. That leaves between eleven and sixteen years to live the life you dream after you retire. Are you kidding? This makes me cringe and I question why people accept that this is their lot in life.

Many have said to me, "It's just not my time."

Hey, if you're alive … *it's your time.*

It's Time

*T*he clock on the wall ticked a countdown to impending doom as we waited for the neurologist to see us. So much had happened—so many tests and appointments—since my diagnosis of Vascular Ehlers-Danlos (vEDS), a serious syndrome that can weaken the major arteries causing aneurysms. But this appointment was by far the scariest of them all.

Life, much like travel, is full of moments, memories, milestones, and mishaps. An introspective reckoning of what truly matters is abundantly clear when you hit your 50s and beyond. Time speeds up, or so it seems. Yet nothing has changed, except us. There comes a point when we reach our wisdom years—we've attained deeper insight and knowledge that only time can give us. These experiences create the patchwork quilt of our lives, shaping who we become.

During the wisdom years, we are free at last and it's time to do the things we only ever dared to dream. Life becomes filled with excitement and questions. It's that pivotal point in life when we want to travel or do something new, maybe try a nomad lifestyle, with no overwhelming responsibilities. This is our time and we've earned it. We all know if we don't act now, time will run out. It's time to act despite the cards being dealt. Or, perhaps more importantly—because of the cards being dealt.

That day came for me.

August 2015 had been unseasonably hot for Canada. As my husband Michael and I walked up the stairs of the medical building, the heat created an illusion of a mirage ahead. Mercifully, we entered the building, and a blast of cool air greeted us. Upon checking in at registration, the nurse told us to take a seat and that we wouldn't have to wait too long.

Two months earlier, my neurologist sent me for an MRI to rule out aneurysms in my noggin, as my mom used to call it; that term somehow making my brain less terrifying to contemplate now. The cursed ticking clock wasn't helping as it continued to remind me of where we were. My anxiety grew with each passing second. Waiting to learn the results from the MRI felt as though someone was standing on my chest.

It's one thing to have two aneurysms on your aorta, but aneurysms in the noggin—not so much. I call my aorta my heart hose. While aneurysms in the heart hose are repairable or even replaceable, noggin aneurysms are not so easily fixed and are far more problematic.

The nurse ushered us into a large room, where various certificates and degrees covered one wall. A large, beautiful ornate oak desk sat in front of three bookcases filled with books on noggins. I wondered if my doctor had read all these books that were so impressively displayed. Behind the desk, between the bookcases, sat an executive-style brown leather high-back swivel chair. Two inviting upholstered occasional chairs sat across from the desk, arranged in what appeared to be optimum distance for conversation.

The sun flooded the room, highlighting the various models of the perfectly placed (albeit macabre) brain puzzles on display—pieces ready to be disassembled and reassembled in the correct noggin configuration. An antiseptic smell filled my nostrils and, again, I became aware of a ticking clock.

Usually, seeing sunlight streaming through a window lifts my mood. But today, the peaceful warmth of the room did little to ease my sense of doom. How could it? This was no ordinary day and my sense of mortality loomed, no matter how sunny the moment.

As we sat in silence, with only the sound of the clock relentlessly screaming *tick, tick, tick*, my mind raced with *what-ifs*. I was about to get up to start pacing when I heard the click of the door handle. And there he was, wearing a spotless white lab coat and perfectly polished loafers, Dr. Anderson.

He entered the room and sat behind the enormous desk in his calfskin brown leather swivel chair. I had the feeling this chair, like the walls, had many stories to tell. How often did he have to give news no one wanted to hear? Too many times, I imagined. I took a deep breath and exhaled slowly to calm my imagination and nerves.

He was measured and cordial, asking me how I was. I responded in kind. My heart began racing, pounding so hard I could hear it. Dr. Anderson didn't let on if he noticed my trembling hands. It was as though it was just another ordinary day, but it wasn't. Indeed, pleasantries were of no need now; I just wanted to know.

He sat forward in his chair. Although I took his posture as a gesture of kindness, I wasn't looking for a casual, friendly conversation. I just wanted to know if my noggin was in trouble. Maybe, the news was good; perhaps there was nothing remarkable to report.

That's what physicians tend to say to you when things are normal. It's always struck me as odd. Why isn't being healthy very remarkable? And yet, in the practice of medicine, it's best to find "nothing remarkable" with a patient. That pronouncement is apparently the golden ticket to health.

My heart rate seemed to slow down with each deep breath I took. *It must be good news*, I silently repeated to myself. *There must be no aneurysms in the noggin, right?* I mean, no self-respecting neurologist would enter the room in such a positive manner should the news be bad.

Dr. Anderson shared the details of my noggin condition meticulously, as revealed by the MRI. There was no mention of impending doom but there was also no mention of "nothing remarkable." After twenty minutes of Dr. Anderson explaining the results, my panic rose again. I could no longer wait; I needed to know. Was there, in fact, something remarkable in my noggin or not?

And, just like that, I blurted it out. "So, I don't have a brain aneurysm." OMG, I wanted to take the words back so I didn't jinx myself. Holding my breath, and hoping my family doctor had been wrong about everything I had going on inside me, I waited. He finished his thought about my continued success in keeping my blood pressure down, which he reminded me was critical for my aorta. And in the next breath, the train hit me full-on.

"Yes, Mrs. Dibblee, you have an aneurysm over your right optic nerve, affecting your vision." He conveyed this news matter-of-factly, as if he had said, "Why, yes, the sky is blue."

Just as I had feared, there *was* something remarkable to report. The alarm bells and lights were all ringing in my head. After that, Michael asked the questions. My anxiety had completely taken over. I could hear them talking but it was as though I was in a tunnel; it all sounded so distant. I wanted to ask questions but I couldn't form a coherent thought. Instead, I focused on a piece of lint on the carpet. It was so seemingly out of place, much like the aneurysm in my noggin.

I came back to my senses on hearing Dr. Anderson telling Michael, "It's time for her to smell the flowers. Don't wait."

That was the day I knew the stirrings I'd felt in my soul were real. I was fifty-five. This deep calling had started five years earlier. Now, the calling, which was more like constant screaming, was saying, "For the love of all that is holy, don't wait any longer."

The Siphonophore

*O*ur decision to winter in Mexico had been set in motion a few months before Dr. Anderson told my husband it was time for me to smell the flowers, *while I can*. It all started in April 2015, when Michael, now a retired firefighter but still an adrenaline junkie and crazy adventurer, traveled to La Ventana in Baja California Sur, Mexico, to learn kiteboarding. He had no idea he was headed for an epic battle of the sea.

Ever since retiring, Michael wanted to learn how to kiteboard. And La Ventana, on the Gulf of California, also known as the Sea of Cortez or the Vermilion Sea, is one of the best places to learn in Mexico. I'd never heard of this extreme sport until one day out of the blue he declared he was going to learn kiteboarding. "To what?" I asked.

Visualize someone on a specialized surf board, who is being propelled on the sea by a giant kite catching the blustery winds. Their feet are strapped to a board, and as their kite flies overhead, they maneuver levers used to power up or down the kite. Many who try this sport give up because of the obstacles they navigate while learning. There's a steep learning curve because much of the process is counterintuitive. Powering up your kite in strong winds can lead to "kitemares." Yes, kitemares are real, along with the walk of shame, the endless mishaps, falling, and getting back up. Kiteboarding isn't for the faint of heart.

Kiteboarding, and the similar sport of kitesurfing, is a fast-growing, extreme water sport in Baja that attracts enthusiasts from around the globe, and for good reason. If you can snow ski, skateboard, or water ski, you can likely learn to kiteboard, but the art takes practice—and lots of it. Even the most accomplished athletes initially find mastering kiteboarding frustrating; thinking it looks as easy as flying a kite on land. But for most who stick with it, finally, there comes a day when everything you've learned clicks in. And off you go, soaring on the wind, sometimes as high as 9 meters (30 feet).

During his trip, Michael spent three weeks going out daily to gain as much knowledge as possible. As an accomplished athlete, he had confidence, which he would later say was a valuable attitude to have. Back in Canada, I received daily emails about his adventures. Some days, Michael's notes were full of optimism and confidence; other days, he expressed frustration and doubt. Yet, he remained determined.

As accomplished athletes are apt to, he thought it should take him less time to learn the basics. After all, he excelled at any sport he tried. Michael perceived this to be a lack of progress and frustration weighed on him. On those days, he said he may have underestimated how difficult this sport was to learn. There were many days Michael wanted to quit. But he didn't. With one week remaining to refine his technique, he felt sure he was ready to stand on his board; to launch. He hoped the favorable winds would continue as the seasons were already changing.

He diligently checked the forecast for wind speeds and best times each night. The season was shifting from spring to summer, which meant the winds were becoming elusive. Eventually, there would be no winds until late fall. Michael wrote that he was hopeful the winds would blow for just one more week.

The following day, he woke to a slight breeze but no wind. By 10:00 a.m., it was scorching hot. Although the winds were slowly picking up, Michael, instead of gearing up for kiting, decided to make it a beach day and relax seaside. As hopeful kiters readied their gear by noon, the offshore winds competed with the day's heat.

He decided it was time to watch and learn from the other kiters in action. Michael found the perfect place to sit and observe the most seasoned kiters dance with the wind, gliding, jumping, and landing with precision while turning into the wind once again. As he watched, he knew he'd master the art and sport of kiting one day. But first, it was time for a swim in the inviting rollers that were breaking into the shore.

As he dove into the turquoise water of the Sea of Cortez to cool down, he instantly felt excruciating pain. When he surfaced, Michael discovered tentacles wrapped about his head, neck, face, arms, and chest. The pain was searing, like nothing he had ever felt. He knew he had to quickly get out of the water and back to the beach.

As he stumbled ashore, Michael attempted to remove the attached wrapped tentacles. The relentless stinging intensified. Instead of falling away from his body, the remaining tentacles continued to grip him and release their deadly venom. Based on the number and length of the tentacles wrapped around him, he knew he had dived into a Portuguese man-of-war. It had stung him repeatedly but he didn't know what would happen next. As he dropped to the sand, he knew he needed help.

The Portuguese man-of-war, or Bluebottle, is often mistakenly referred to as a jellyfish. But it isn't a jellyfish—it's a siphonophore. Siphonophores are a colony of separate organisms working together as one with tentacles that can exceed 46 meters (150 feet) below the surface. And they are found in every ocean except the Arctic.

These organisms propel through ocean currents because of their inflated bladder—resembling an ancient warship at full sail. They are sea predators, with venom-filled tendrils paralyzing their prey. Although the sting of a siphonophore is rarely fatal in humans, when someone tangles with the Portuguese man-of-war, the sting is excruciating and can leave lifelong scarring.

Within minutes, Michael's body was suffering the effects of the venom and he went into shock. His body couldn't handle the amount of toxic venom injected. Luckily, a groundskeeper saw him lying outside, recognized the sting's effects, and got him to a doctor for immediate treatment. Upon arriving at the clinic in La Ventana, the doctor told him it was the worst sting he had seen in twenty-five years.

The doctor also said it was rare to have a Portuguese man-of-war so close to shore. He attributed their arrival to the recent southwesterly winds and currents they had been experiencing the last week. Michael was in tough shape. The excess venom load caused disorientation, fever, and exhaustion. With each passing hour, his symptoms worsened.

That night, I received my daily update via email. It read, "Today, I didn't go kiting, a Portuguese man-of-war stung me, and it's horrible." I sat reading the email over and over. What did this mean? I responded to his email but had no response. There was no phone service where Michael was staying. Two days later, I received a call from his brother, Bruce, who was on vacation with Michael. Bruce explained everything, told me Michael was doing well, and not to worry.

It would be another ninety-six hours before I would speak to Michael. When we finally talked by phone, he didn't sound like himself at all; his voice was raspy and weak. Michael assured me he'd be fine and there was no need for me to come to Mexico. I decided to wait until he returned home to ask *all* my questions. He was alive, and that was the only thing that mattered at the moment.

It would be ten more days until I set my eyes on Michael. He looked as though he had suffered severe burns and lashes across his face, neck, chest, and most predominantly, his ears. Within minutes of getting off the ferry, he said, "I know you'd love the Baja. It's beautiful; we need to make a plan."

I thought he was out of his mind. He'd just had a dangerous encounter with a sea creature. It would take months for the wounds to heal. At that moment, I wasn't very open to wintering in Baja, or anywhere else, given what had just happened.

But my initial trepidation and fear eased over the next few months as Michael painted the idyllic picture of warm beach days, delicious cuisine, a culture I loved, and no rain or snow for months. The Portuguese man-o-war had beaten him up but it hadn't killed his love of Mexico!

How to Treat a Portuguese Man-Of-War Sting

There are two effective ways to self-treat the stings, yet there is a lot of misinformation that circulates after an attack. The myths and tales of the sea often carry stories from one generation to another. These folklores are dangerous and can cause more harm than good. Here are a few of the various "treatment" tales:

» Scrape the stingers. No! Do not scrape the stingers, as this spreads the venom.

» Rinse the area with fresh water or seawater. This seems logical but has no effect and does nothing to stop the poison from continuing to be released.

» Pour on alcohol or ethanol ammonia. No! This will only further burn the skin and agitate the barbs.

» Cover the wound with gauze. Don't do this. Dark, damp environments encourage more toxins to be released. Nor should you rub the area with a towel or anything that serves only to agitate and cause them to release more venom.

» Pull the tentacles off your body. No! Never do this. If you must touch the tentacles, wear gloves to prevent them from spreading more toxins.

Oh, and then there are these two personal favorites:

» Pee on them. *No, thank you.*

» Apply meat tenderizer. No! You are not cooking a steak. Do not do this.

So, how should you treat a Portuguese man-of-war sting? With an ingredient found in almost every kitchen: vinegar. First, pour vinegar over the area to neutralize the venom's barbs and impact. Next, soak the affected area in hot water for twenty to forty-five minutes. Next, seek immediate medical attention, as the reaction is different for each person and the amount of poison determines the response.

Should I Stay or Should I Go?

*M*ichael is persuasive when he's determined. One morning over breakfast, Michael spoke about how much he'd enjoyed learning to kite every day. His only regret was that he couldn't complete the last week. He told me about all the amazing people he'd met while taking lessons. He had found a new sport that was both exhilarating and terrifying. (Did I mention he's also a former bull rider?) His enthusiasm and conviction to improve his Spanish skills while spending a winter in Baja with me was infectious.

While he remained laser-focused on wintering in Baja, I was reluctantly processing the idea, because he was still healing from the attack. But as most of the lash wounds healed as the weeks passed, I became less hesitant and more curious. We entered the possibility of maybe.

I had run my speaking and event-planning business from Canada and Montana for years, but Mexico was an unknown. I knew there were inherent internet challenges in Mexico, and for me to run my business, I needed dependable internet. There were many other moving parts and pieces to consider. Maybe Michael could go and I could visit every month? Or we'd go for three months instead of six, to test drive living seaside in a tiny home while running my business?

My thoughts shifted to *should I stay or should I go?* The thoughts about the possibility and opportunities to do more meaningful and impactful volunteer work were intriguing. And what about family? I adore my children and grandchildren. Our plan would require factoring in family time, traveling during Christmas, holidays, and other milestone dates. But how? Plus, none of this would matter if I couldn't pivot my business to run from Mexico.

Soon enough, I was on a discovery mission. Every day, we looked online for places that offered kiteboarding and community. However, we both knew spending months in another country would require finding more than food, surf, and sand.

I hadn't seen Michael this excited since his retirement in 2012. Every time he shared something; his face beamed with an ear-to-ear smile. It was almost impossible to resist his youthful enthusiasm. Although I was softening to the idea of wintering in Mexico, I still had concerns about my business.

If we were to live in the Baja during the winter, two caveats were important to me. We'd commit to returning to Canada for two weeks to spend Christmas with the grandchildren and have time with friends over the season. And, if I wanted to return for a family visit anytime, that wouldn't be an issue. Michael completely understood how vital these caveats were to me. Although we lived on Vancouver Island in British Columbia, the majority of our family lived in Alberta. I couldn't fathom being so far away for such a long period. Once I knew he understood my concerns and agreed we'd accommodate trips home, I was all in.

We continued to look online for the perfect seaside villages to explore and read about what to expect when wintering in Baja. As an author and event planner, it's possible to operate my business online anywhere, as long as I have good internet service. Internet in Mexico isn't the same as Canada. Live streaming and video conferencing calls are often challenging. But I was confident there would be a solution. And there was, but it took some time to figure it out.

Michael initially wanted to return to La Ventana, but he knew the community lacked the amenities and necessities I needed. So, we decided to fly in late June 2015 for a Baja scouting trip to find the perfect winter location. If all worked out, we'd drive to Mexico in November with our tiny home in tow to set up camp for the winter.

We continued to research from Canada, looking for a resort to use as a base camp, as this was much easier than moving from town to town. Since we were drawn to small seaside villages on the Sea of Cortez, we quickly ruled out places that didn't fit. Never before had I decided where to stay based on the wind, but this condition was essential for Michael to continue his quest of mastering kiteboarding. And I could just buy more hairspray!

Our research file grew thicker by the day. I sensed something significant was going to happen in our not-to-distant future. Michael's enthusiasm was infectious and now I, too, was dreaming of all the possibilities. A couple of Canadian kids—living in Mexico!

Our Wish Lists

Michael's criteria for the perfect windy getaway:

- » Small seaside community on the Sea of Cortez.
- » Wind on most days from December through March.
- » Spanish speaking community.
- » Proximity to La Paz and Los Cabos.
- » Warm evenings from January through March.
- » Beach access.
- » Paddleboarding.
- » Snorkeling.

My criteria were only slightly different:

- » A small community on the Sea of Cortez.
- » Internet.
- » Proximity to La Paz and Los Cabos.
- » Ability to learn Spanish.
- » Places to volunteer.
- » Access to safe swimming beaches.
- » Paddleboarding.
- » Snorkeling.
- » Access to grocery stores.
- » Proximity to an international airport.

The Best Kiteboarding Places
in the Baja California Peninsula

Bajar is the Spanish verb "to lower" and Baja California is considered lower California. We made a list of ideal kiting locations in the area, based on consistent wind conditions.

La Ventana (The Window). This small but quaint seaside village is haled as the number one spot for kiteboarding and kitesurfing in Baja. Wind dominates the season, leaving little to no paddle boarding or snorkeling. La Ventana's location to an international airport is a minimum two-hour drive. It also lacked some of the other amenities I was seeking.

Los Barriles (The Barrels). Charming, and slightly bigger than La Ventana, Los Barriles offers more of everything, including days without wind for paddleboarding and snorkeling. The population doubles over the winter months with Canadians and Americans. Still, Los Barriles remains true to its Spanish heritage. With mostly sand streets, drivable arroyos, small taquerias, restaurants, accommodations, a strong core community of locals and expats, plus volunteer opportunities, Los Barriles was a draw for both of us.

Bahia Santa Maria. Although rated an excellent place for kiters, we quickly ruled Santa Maria out since it was too far north of where we wanted to be and the beaches were primarily rocky.

San Juanico (Scorpion Bay). This is a tiny fishing village with limited amenities. Also, it's located too far north of La Paz and Los Cabos. The water is recommended by surfers; however, the wind is inconsistent and presents high risks for beginners.

Punta Abreojos. This isolated fishing town looked very promising. But it isn't on the Sea of Cortez so we didn't explore the option of this community.

But It All Changed

$\mathcal{W}$e traveled to Alberta in late May 2015 to visit family and friends and share our winter plans with them. The reception wasn't as enthusiastic as we thought it would be. It ranged from fear for our safety to terror. We understood why since the Canadian media often broadcasts negative news stories about Mexico's drug cartels. We knew everyone would feel better once they knew we were in a safe location. It was time to solidify a plan of some sort.

But on June 21, 2015, everything changed!

While we were in Alberta, Michael went for his annual medical check-up with the Calgary Fire Department Wellness clinic. His blood test relieved his Prostate-Specific Antigen (PSA) levels were far too high, a key indicator of prostate cancer. He needed to see a specialist as soon as we returned to Vancouver Island. This meant cutting our trip short and driving back home, some thirteen hours through mountain passes, plus a ferry ride. It was terrifying not knowing what the diagnosis meant and yet knowing we were facing something serious.

For the next few months, we put everything on hold. A month or so later, on August 12, we got the news no one wanted. After tests and more tests, it was confirmed; Michael had prostate cancer and would need immediate surgical intervention to save his life. This was not about early intervention. It was way past that. The message was: act now, or you will die. It was terrifying and there were no guarantees. But without surgery, he would not make it long. By all indications, the cancer was spreading fast.

When we met with the urologist, his first words after introducing himself were, "Michael, you are in for the fight of your life." We both sat in silence, gob smacked. *How could this be?* Dr. MacCracken said Michael needed an immediate procedure called a radical prostatectomy. This procedure would give him a fifty-fifty chance of survival. The treatment would slow the spread of cancer but would not cure him.

What? How could this be?

Dr. MacCracken went through what needed to happen in the next few weeks; none of which sounded promising. Michael's surgery was scheduled for September. From that moment on, we were smack dab in the middle of the muck and mire. Every test Michael took came back more damaging than the last. We continued to hope for a good outcome but cancer is brutal and doesn't discriminate.

The surgery revealed the cells had spread to two of his lymph nodes and beyond. The operation was radical and lifesaving. I felt utterly incompetent. I knew there was nothing I could do, but I wanted to make it better.

By Christmas, things were improving, Michael's PSA levels were stabilizing, and they began to trend down. After getting clearance from the doctor, we decided to take a short trip to Mexico for a couple of weeks. We needed a break from the muck and mire. Dr. MacCracken advised us, "Go, *while you can.*" This phase was becoming too familiar.

It wasn't for long, but it helped us refocus and recenter. We knew when we returned Michael had both radiation and hormone treatment awaiting him. We decided to focus on the positive and have a great time. We did. We purposely didn't go to Baja. We didn't want cancer to be a part of our Baja dream. Instead, we traveled to Riviera Nayarit, Mexico, not far from Puerto Vallarta, and treated ourselves to an all-inclusive five-star resort. We were finally able to exhale and return to our dream that had been shockingly interrupted. Once again, we began visualizing a life wintering in Baja.

When we arrived back in Canada, Michael completed all the recommended treatments. Thankfully, the good news of recovery continued. By May 2016, Dr. MacCracken said Michael would still require monthly tests but he felt strongly Michael was now in remission. Remission is a beautiful word, filled with promise.

We fired up our Sea of Cortez research again, hopeful he would continue to heal. That winter, we returned for another short visit to Mexico for a December break, again steering clear of Baja.

It would be almost two years before we would make our long-planned scouting trip to Baja. By then, we were ready to make our dream a reality. Cancer—or any life-threatening illness—taught us that life is precarious and ever-changing. Although we had to navigate some rough seas, we stayed committed and never forgot what Dr. MacCracken said.

"Go, *while you can*."

The Window or The Barrels?

*I*n June 2017, we arrived in Cabo San Lucas, Baja California Sur, Mexico. Although I'd been to other areas in Mexico before, Baja was new to me, but anywhere in Mexico in June is vastly different from December. The humidity hits you as soon as the door opens. And not in a gentle, kind, dewy way; instead, it's an oh-my-God-it-is-so-hot-and-sticky kind of way.

Leaving the comfortable climate-controlled plane to descend onto the searing hot tarmac, a wall of intense heat assaults the body. It's as though you've walked into a sauna. Every step taken on the asphalt to the terminal is energy-depleting. The body can't adjust quickly enough to the dramatic change in temperature and humidity. By the time I entered the air-conditioned terminal, I was dripping. I was never so grateful for air conditioning!

Once inside, the coolness provided immediate relief. We both looked at each other simultaneously, grinning ear to ear. With a quick fist bump and a collective sigh of relief, both from the heat and the last two years battling health issues, we knew we had made it through to the other side. We were here, at last, and we were both excited.

The next stop was the resort. After a brief stop to pick up our rental car, we arrived at a primarily empty hotel. Visiting in June is great for that. Once settled in, we decided we needed a couple of days to solidify our plan to tour La Ventana and Los Barriles, and to visit Todos Santos and the beaches.

Before we left Canada, we decided we'd begin in La Ventana and make our way back south to Los Barriles. I felt certain Los Barriles would best serve us both. Sitting in Canada with all my creature comforts, sipping my tea while surfing the internet, and researching the recommended villages was pretty straightforward. Now, *this* was real.

Naturally, our plans changed once we arrived. The challenges of working in another country surfaced almost immediately through language. Michael had a rudimentary understanding of Spanish, but I didn't. We figured things out as one does when you're in another country, and thank goodness for the Google Translate app.

On day three, we left just after sunrise and headed north along the Transpeninsular Highway, first to the furthest point away which is La Paz, meaning The Peace. There, we took a tea break, then refueled and turned south on Highway 286 to La Ventana. As we drove the windy roads in our compact rental car, we saw firsthand the obstacles we'd face when towing our tiny home on wheels.

We encountered burros, lots of cows, goats, and real-life roadrunners. Beep! Beep! The landscape was so varied and like nothing I'd ever imagined. Far beyond the stereotypical representations of a Mexico filled with cactus and deserts, here the landscape was picturesque and resilient, beautiful, yet harsh and unforgiving.

As I sat in the passenger seat, the diversity amazed me. How had I not known this? We descended to the desert landscape and the oasis from the majestic mountain pass. Yes, an oasis in the turquoise Sea of Cortez.

We arrived in La Ventana by late morning. Although I felt confident, and therefore biased, toward Los Barriles from my research, I wanted to keep an open mind. I've lived in many towns and I know when the feeling of belonging greets me.

As we entered La Ventana, located about forty minutes south of La Paz on the eastern side of the Baja California Peninsula, Michael seamlessly shifted from driver to tour guide. He called out every point of interest we passed. The memories quickly transported him back to the weeks in 2015 when he took his kiteboarding lessons.

"This is where the cow was eating the cardboard pizza box," he stated, laughing. "And right here is a perfect place for the tiny home," he told me, although it would require us to "rough camp," as I called it.

Here, only the essential amenities would be accessible. Rough camping is one step up from boondocking. To "boondock" is to camp old-style, off the grid on public lands, in the middle of nowhere, with no hookups, electricity, sewage, water—nothing. The ability to be completely self-sufficient is a must. However, in my wisdom years, I prefer "glamping" with some of my creature comforts: tea and toast, flushing toilets, showering indoors, and mostly living in a proper home, only on wheels.

As you enter La Ventana from the south, on the right there is beach access to a local campground that Michael was excited to show me, which offered essential services—including electricity and water—but no onsite sewage access. He declared, "This is the one I was telling you about. This is where we could spend the winter if we were to come to La Ventana." It was named Campground del Ejido de La Ventana y El Sargento. The proximity to the beach was certainly appealing.

Before leaving Canada, we'd spoken to a few people about our plans and the message was clear: if you're a kiter or interested in being a kiter, La Ventana is the place to be because the winds are consistent for months. *Months.* I realized this meant a lot to Michael.

The winds begin in the late morning and often blow until late afternoon—every day. Initially, the winds are a welcome reprieve from the heat and humidity of summer, but soon the winds become a non-kiters bane of existence and frustration. Living beachside means enjoying the outdoors, not sitting in a tiny home for endless days, waiting for the wind to subside. Further, for non-kiters, the wind's velocity becomes a challenge and creates a state of constant clean-up as debris blows from other sites and off the beach.

Although I was open to living in the tiny home, I wasn't interested in sheltering from the wind for hours and days at a time. Though beautiful in so many respects, La Ventana offered limited amenities and lacked some basic creature comforts including grocery stores and internet availability. Plus, the ongoing winds, and my allergies, did nothing to convince me this was to be our home over the winter.

A few dedicated campers remained seaside-living year-round on the beach. Since the wind is almost nonexistent from late spring through fall, those waiting for kiting again enjoy paddleboarding and long, hazy beach days. I wondered who could afford this nomadic lifestyle? Some people could, and they were there. And we were merely exploring the possibility.

If our only interest was mastering kiting, La Ventana would be the place to be for wintering. It ticked many of the boxes on our desire list, but I needed more: more community, more flexibility, and more creature comforts. When we left La Ventana, my excitement and bias grew. Having now seen La Ventana and confirming its limitations, I was confident Los Barriles was to be "our place."

As we made our way through the mountain pass, we saw in the distance a large object. It wasn't until we were much closer that I recognized it: La Romana of El Triunfo, known as the smokestack. I had read about this smokestack but hadn't grasped its actual size. It projects so high that it appears to reach the sky. At a whopping 47 meters (154 feet) tall, it towers over everything else as far as the eyes can see. Local legend is that Gustav Eiffel, the man behind the Eiffel Tower in Paris, was the designer.

On our way to the small colonial town, we drove through the mountains of Sierra de la Laguna. Arriving in El Triunfo, which translates to The Triumph, felt like stumbling upon a secret garden. Designated as a biosphere reserve, El Triunfo sits between the Pacific Ocean and the Grijalva-Usumacinta River at 457 meters (1,500 feet) above sea level. The reserve is an endemic area for different plants and animals and Mexico's most diverse evergreen cloud forest. Rich in history, the town is best described as a step back in time. It's a beautiful oasis in the middle of nowhere that draws you in immediately.

El Triunfo had come up several times when I began researching La Ventana and Los Barriles. It's nestled in the mountains and is not to be missed. El Triunfo has a history of both boom-and-bust times. Once, it was a thriving gold and silver mining town with more than 10,000 residents. Now, it's been designated a historic landmark in Baja, and only a few hundred people call it home.

The charm of El Triunfo is everywhere and easy to see with freshly-restored, stained, and painted hand-carved heavy wooden doors featuring wrought iron details and hardware. And, as if on cue, the quintessential scene played out before us. An older Mexican gentleman sat on a carved and colorful wooden bench, reminding me of the many travel ads I had seen in the past. We both wanted to stop and take in everything El Triunfo offered, but today wasn't the day.

As we continued our day of exploration with anticipation, we passed many villages along the way, vowing to check them out in the future. Once again, the windy, arid, desert road and terrain gave way to lush green rainforests abundant with life. We both realized if we hadn't driven, we would have missed the experience of the true beauty of Baja.

Forty-five minutes later, we arrived in Los Barriles. The entrance greets you from the highway, with barrel fountains welcoming tourists and residents alike into the once sleepy fishing village.

Los Barriles is part of Baja's East Cape region. The Pacific Ocean and the Sea of Cortez meet at the southernmost tip of Baja, and Los

Barriles is some 111 kilometers (69 miles) north and east of San José del Cabo on the Sea of Cortez. We know it now for its unspoiled vistas, stunning crystal-clear turquoise waters, world-class windsurfing, kite-boarding, diving, snorkeling, and sportfishing.

As we entered Los Barriles, we immediately noticed the multiple ATVs on the road, which far outnumbered cars. Even more surprising were the number of ATVs on the beach. Los Barriles is where adventure meets charm. Here is where we found the balance I was seeking: white-sand beaches and streets bustling with traditional shops, restaurants, and services. Everything about Los Barriles said yes; we were both sure we had found our place!

Unlike other fishing villages in Mexico that haven't grown much in the last several decades, Los Barriles offers many amenities. Yet, the town remains intact and not overrun by large commercial buildings that tower over mom-and-pop stores. Indeed, we could see Los Barriles offered everything we needed regarding services and access. There were multiple banks, a hardware store, a second-hand store, a consignment store, two full-size grocery stores, and the list went on. Although worlds apart from the hustle and bustle of Cabo San Lucas, we were happy to find that Los Barriles offers something for almost everyone.

It had been a long and productive day, but we still wanted to explore the RV parks and ensure internet access. Although there were three RV park contenders, only two were on the beach, which was on our must-have list, but only one offered internet access. I explained to the park manager my need for accessible and dependable internet, and he assured me this wouldn't be a problem, even offering to boost the signal if need be.

Los Barriles ticked *every* box. So sure were we that we had found our perfect piece of beach heaven, we put a deposit on Site Number

Six. Suddenly, things got real. We committed to arriving in the first week of November and staying until mid-March.

At that moment, it was both real and surreal. We were going to do this! We both wanted to pull up some chairs to sit in our empty Number Six, enjoy the sunset, and watch the Sea of Cortez roll in and out. But we knew we needed to leave before dusk. One thing we had discovered while researching—and later reinforced to us by nearly everyone we met—was never to drive in the dark. However, we did not yet know why, but we would soon learn.

We were excited as we pulled out of the RV park that beautiful sunny afternoon, waving goodbye to the park manager and the sea. We had so many ideas and realized we had so much to do. Suddenly, my head filled with more questions than answers about how and what we would need. I thought, *this couldn't be that hard, could it?* After all, hundreds of thousands of people do this every year! It's not like we were pioneers or breaking new ground. Still ...

The warm afternoon light of the sun created a golden hue on everything, as if in approval of our decision. We were both in a state of wonderment and anticipation of all that was to come as we made the long drive back to our hotel, darkness nearly upon us.

Just as we were about to enter the city limits of San Jose del Cabo, I saw the herd. This was not wild deer, elk, or moose, like we see sometimes on highways in Canada. Nope, this was a herd of cows, followed by some goats, and, wait for it: A BURRO. It was something to behold.

They warn you not to drive at night, and now we understand why. There are no fences to contain livestock, so they freely move in search of food and water. Even more problematic are cows that don't move quickly. Some appear to enjoy the heat of the pavement and decide to lie down in the middle of the road; vehicles and sleeping cows don't make for favorable outcomes.

We arrived at the resort full of ideas and questions. But knowing we had found and secured Number Six made it real and all the more exciting. We used the rest of our trip to do more exploring in other areas, and looked into what we would require for wintering in Mexico. The days flew by and our anticipation grew. When we left for home, we knew we wouldn't be gone long.

Best Laid Plans

*O*ver the following months, we prepared for our epic road trip from Canada to Los Barriles. We informed our family and friends this was happening! Once again, concerns and fears for our safety were topics of discussion. We, too, had seen the horrendous news reports of danger and retaliation of the Cartel in Juarez. Mexican cartels deal in ruthless justice. The media doesn't often share the context and location of these horrific and tragic events, but their crimes are well documented and exploited in movies and on television.

First, we explained, Los Barriles is nowhere near the Ciudad of Juarez, which is in Chihuahua, Mexico. To get an idea of the distance, it would be like saying Kenora, Ontario is next to Vancouver, British Columbia, or Detroit, Michigan is next to Seattle, Washington. Although both places are in the same country, they are nowhere near each other, and would take days of driving to reach either one. Next, the Sea of Cortez separates the Baja Peninsula from the mainland.

Their concern was based on reports of widespread violence and caused them considerable angst. We did our best to quell their fears, but perception is difficult to dispute. So, we committed to sharing our phone location while driving to help ease their concerns and agreed to daily check-ins. Even though cell coverage would be sparse in some parts, this safety step did help in reducing their fears.

We started with Plan A; by the time we were ready to leave, it was Plan L. "Los Barriles or Bust" became our daily mantra as our lists grew longer each day.

According to online map apps, Site Number Six was a forty-seven-hour drive. We had 4,009 kilometers (2,492 miles) ahead of us. Based on driving eleven-hour days, which accounted for breaks and towing; we estimated we could reach Number Six in a very ambitious five-day span.

Yes, five days. We both loved long road trips and windshield time, and we had traveled many times to the southern United States from Canada. We had no way of knowing what we did not know; our first lesson from the epic road trip!

Most things in life must be experienced and learned; there's no shortcut or free pass. It is from these moments we know and do better, or, at the very least, become wiser. It wasn't as though we hadn't done our research and talked to others, but there were plenty of things we did not, or could not, know.

We didn't know about or consider the hundred-year rains. How could we? There is an average of only 41 centimeters (16 inches) of rain per year in Baja. Contrary to popular belief, the hundred-year rains don't happen every one hundred years. There's only a one percent chance and we hit it! Our truck and trailer turned into an ark.

Nor did we allow for the time to cross two different borders with different requirements and rules. Instead, we followed the "on a need-to-know basis" mentality. We'd address whatever we needed to do as the situation dictated. What we needed was to keep our eye on the prize.

The verb for "to need" in Spanish is *necesitar*. When conjugated it's "I need," *necesito*, and "you need," *necesitas*. These became essential words to know.

As a young girl, I dreamt of going on epic road trips to exotic lands. And here we were, Mia Mukluks, our beloved pooch, Grumpy Tequila, the cat, and the two Traveling Fools, my husband and myself, about to embark on our epic journey. The focus was on arriving safe and sound.

After speaking with many who had driven the long haul south from western Canada to Mexico, a common theme emerged: taking US 101 along the coastline through Washington, Oregon, and parts of California is a must. This meant more research, but I was up for the challenge.

It took me no time to see why driving this coastal highway came highly recommended. The consensus was to take this road if you love coastal routes with breathtaking views. Who doesn't? Epic road trips aren't simply about point A to point B. Indeed, epic road trips need vistas and moments that capture your heart.

The coastal route Highway 101 through Washington and Oregon, would add 800 to 965 kilometers (500 to 600 miles) to our road trip. Was the extra mileage and time worth it? Yes, of course! Bring on the coastal views!

And we were now that much closer to the big Mexican move.

⁓✏⁓

Plan B

Alternatively, we could travel south on Interstate 5, the fastest north-south highway running inland and parallel to the Pacific Ocean. I-5 begins at the Peace Arch Crossing in Canada (Highway 99) and ends at the United States-Mexico border in San Ysidro.

I-5 is the only continuous highway that touches both the Canadian and Mexican borders and is approximately 2,300 kilometers (1,429 miles) long. Once crossing into Baja, Mexico, you can branch out onto Mexico Federal Highways 1 and 10, following the coastline again.

The Postage Stamp

*L*eading up to embarking on our epic road trip, we were continuously refining and upgrading our plans. We discovered and implemented things as we prepared. It seemed we'd find our footing and understanding about something, only to learn we'd missed something else. What we thought we understood seemed to change daily. At some point, I don't remember exactly when, we decided we would adapt as needed; maybe this became obvious after we'd changed our plan so many times.

The day in late October of 2017 finally arrived; it was time and we were as ready as we could possibly be. That morning, we woke early, not because we had to, but because we were so excited. Our epic road trip would begin with a ferry to Port Angeles which was leaving at 4:00 p.m. We filled the morning hours with puttering about, checking and rechecking the trailer's contents and our manifest while tying up any loose ends with neighbors.

There wasn't an inch to spare; we were fully loaded. Thank goodness we had a big truck with a mega cab, but even so, space was tight. Packing up became a game of Tetra Block. We began by folding the backseats down to create a flat surface. On top of that, we placed our two, fully-loaded, 23-kilogram (50-pound) suitcases. On top of these, we placed and secured the crates for Grumpy Tequila, our feisty cat, and for Mia Mukluks, our rescue pup, to give them optimal viewing perches and cool air circulation.

Behind my seat, we loaded my desktop computer, two briefcases, and a cooler. We used every available space; even the roof of the cab became valuable space for hauling. There, we mounted two paddle boards as well as our bicycles. The ATV took up most of the truck bed, along with the generator, four portable jerry cans, and a box of miscellaneous tools and items.

For the last and final step, we hitched the trailer to the truck. The scene was surreal as I stood outside, looking at our home and then the trailer. We were about to leave our 232 square meter (2,500 square foot), five-bedroom home to live in 18 square meters (190 square feet) for up to six months. It was essentially a single room on wheels. One thing was for sure: we would have stories to tell, and likely lots of them!

This was some serious downsizing. While people often romanticize about tiny home living, suffice to say, there is a reason they call it tiny. We named our new home the Postage Stamp. The trailer was designed to live in for two to three weeks, not six months. Living in this miniature house would require compromise, but we were banking on living mostly outside at our campsite, Site Number Six.

Taking one last walk around the truck and the Postage Stamp to ensure everything was in order and measuring for the ferry trip to the mainland, we discovered we were a little bit more than 14 meters (47 feet) in length. We pulled out of the driveway at noon, excited—and maybe a little naïve—about what lay ahead. We were embarking on the most challenging and heart-filling road trip. Plus, having driven class-one vehicles since he was nineteen years old, Michael was confident our rig would pose no problems for him.

The Postage Stamp was considered glamping when compared to tenting, for sure. It could sleep four adults comfortably with two queen beds, but the inside was tight. What it lacked in space, it made up for in small amenities. The compact dinette sat two adults, and we had a tiny sink, a tiny microwave, a small pantry, a small TV, a small refrigerator, and a pint-sized love seat. When fully set up and open, the Stamp resembled a small galley kitchen with a bed at each end.

When we left Canada that day, every cupboard was bursting. We used every available space to take what we were sure we needed, and some things that were nice to have. I spent weeks leading up to our departure strategically narrowing down exactly what I would need to run my business and work from Baja.

I allotted one storage bin to all my must-haves. To ensure everything fit, I packed and repacked the bin repeatedly. By the time we left, I knew its contents intimately; I even started dreaming about it. Clearly, I was ready. I left nothing to chance for what would become my mobile office. Michael even added some bonus shelving for my office supplies over the window above the dinette.

Our family was happy and ready for the road. What more could I ask for? Nothing.

The Black Ball Ferry

As we boarded the Black Ball Ferry from downtown Victoria on Thursday, October 26, 2017, I was in disbelief. Our joint enthusiasm and anticipation grew with each passing minute. The ferry from downtown Victoria to Port Angeles is one of my favorites, offering scenic vistas. I think of the ferry and refer to it as day cruising, and on this day, the weather and sea did not disappoint. It was a breathtaking day cruise.

We docked in Port Angeles, Washington, a charming seaside town. After clearing United States customs, we set out to find a local RV park before nightfall. There was no going back now. Yep, this was it.

Not too much time passed before we found our first RV park. The Seven Cedars Casino offered RV sites and its proximity to the highway made it appealing. We settled in for the night with the realization that the next day would be the beginning of something neither of us had ever done before. It was both terrifying and exhilarating.

We rose early the following morning as we wanted to get a jump-start on the driving. As we exited the parking lot, the sun popped up, as if on cue. Spreading its orange and red hues across the sky and through the trees as if to say, "Get a move on!" And off, we went.

Within minutes, we fully understood the strong advice about taking Highway 101. The coastline road offered the most picturesque seaside vistas I'd ever seen. Just when we thought we had seen the best of the best, we'd see yet another majestic scene playing out as the ocean crashed against the giant boulders. I have deep respect for the ocean; I find it both beautiful and terrifying at the same time when the waves crash into the shore. The power of water is never to be underestimated.

We reached a stretch of Highway 101, called the Olympic Peninsula scenic drive, where the perimeter of the Olympic Peninsula runs through the Hoh Rainforest. This is the largest temperate rainforest in the northwest and averages up to 4 meters (14 feet) of rain a year, resulting in a lush, green canopy of vegetation and an abundance of life. As if dancing in a kaleidoscope of color from the sun, the morning dew produced an eerily sentient mist, creating a divine opening into what appeared to be a medieval forest.

If you have never been to a rainforest, I highly recommend it, as the purpose and evidence of nature working her magic is indisputable. Oh, to walk and be in this moment in nature is the stuff of dreams and healing.

Michael and I marveled at the engineering brilliance it took to build this road, which mostly hugs the shoreline. With its endless views of waves where the sea meets the shore in a beautifully choreographed dance, there are moments of violent force and times of a tender touch.

Little did we know, Highway 101, with its many twists and tight corners, was preparing us for the roads ahead in Mexico. The scenery was spectacular, but there was little to no room for driving error. On a few tight corners, I held my breath and squeezed my eyes tightly. I'm sure Michael heard a few gasps as we passed other oversized oncoming vehicles in those tight turns. Being a passenger with a bird's-eye view has both advantages and disadvantages.

Of the many heart-stirring sea vistas we saw, the iconic and most majestic was Cannon Beach. Haystack Rock, as though divinely placed, captures your attention. Though not a rock at all, Haystack Rock stands 72 meters (235 feet) and is composed of basalts that create a "sea stack," which I can only describe as magnificent. Basalt is the by-product of the rapid cooling of lava on the ocean floor that combines with sediment. Over time, the rocks "stack" in the sea, forming a sea stack.

Haystack Rock juts out of the Pacific Ocean as if rising from the abyss; as tall as a twenty-three-story high-rise, it's really something to see. At first glance, Haystack appears jagged, uninhabitable, and unforgiving. And yet, it's home to many sea birds and creatures with colorful tide pools offering refuge to sea stars, anemones, crabs, chitons, limpets, and nudibranchs. If you time your arrival to Haystack within an hour of low tide, you can walk out and see this wonder of nature.

After a brief stop, we were back on the road again. Our next stop would be an upscale RV park in Lincoln City, Oregon. We discovered Lincoln City when researching possible overnight camping spots, and this town is centrally located on the west coast of Oregon. Our goal was to arrive early enough to take advantage of what Lincoln City offers. The beaches are said to be some of the best in the United States.

Highway 101 runs through Lincoln City, yet there's no sense of hurry. Maybe the miles and miles of white sandy beach change the pace, or the fact the quintessential seaside boutiques—with their quirky and unique wares placed invitingly on the sidewalks—make the town seem so quaint. After a quick setup at the park, we headed to the beach to enjoy and explore.

With miles of sandy beach and views that take your breath away, it was undeniably one of the most beautiful beaches we'd ever seen. The breeze off the ocean and the setting sun as we walked hand in hand down the shoreline—watching Mia Mukluks running into the surf and delighting in every wave—was surreal. I could taste the saltiness of the sea air. Each wave seemed to kiss the shore only to leave and return. It was as though we were playing out a romantic movie scene.

We took our time. And as if nature herself told us to sit a spell, we found a perfectly placed log to watch the waves roll in with the high tide. My heartbeat slowed, and all that truly mattered was in this very moment.

As we walked back to the Postage Stamp, dusk overtook the day, giving us a perfect ending. We made a simple dinner of eggs and buttery-slathered toast, then plotted our next day. From here on, this became our nightly routine during our long trek to Site Number Six. Plotting out the milage, time, and locations, provided context as to how far we had already traveled, and what lay ahead.

The following day, we left for Canyonville, Oregon. Our destination was the Seven Feathers Casino RV Park. We rose early, set the GPS, and headed to Salem, Oregon. As we set out to chase the sunrise to Salem, we talked about all things Salem. This Salem, often confused with the infamous one of the witch hunts in Massachusetts, was lovely and welcoming.

I hoped to visit the Enchanted Forest, which I had only read about. From what I understood, it's a fairy tale village in the forest, and that sounded like a fun adventure. Since I was in the princess seat, (*aka* the passenger seat), I did a little more research and learned it was best to visit when we could spend an entire day there. So, we set this destination aside for another time, perhaps.

One of RVing's many perks is deciding where and how long to stop. Course adjusting is a luxury when you have your tiny home on wheels behind you.

⌇⌇⌇

The Autobahn of Interstate Five

*T*he United States is a conglomerate of freeways that move traffic efficiently. The second most traveled freeway on the west coast running north and south is I-5. Although it runs mainly parallel to the coastline highways, it definitely lacks in scenic beauty. However, what it lacks in beauty it makes up for in access and driving ease.

What surprised us most on I-5 were the rest stops. We have rest stops in Canada, and many are very nice, but these made ours in Canada seem lacking—even rustic. Featuring clean bathrooms, refreshment stands or vending machines, beautifully manicured lawns, off-leash areas, and even freshwater streams at some that Mia Mukluks enjoyed immensely, many American rest stops are inviting and genuinely relaxing.

Along the interstate, commercial truck lanes provide refuge from the speeding drivers, and multiple lanes dramatically help to reduce congestion. There are, of course, exceptions, as we discovered once we crossed into California. As we continued our way south, each day seemed much like the previous one. We would drive up to thirteen hours and park for the night.

We pulled into Los Angeles in the late afternoon on day three. If you've ever driven in LA, you can imagine that traveling with the Postage Stamp in tow was neither ideal nor pragmatic. In some stretches, there are sixteen lanes across. It's more of a motorway, and it's fast—like what I imagine the Autobahn to be in Germany. The posted speed limit is 112 kilometers (70 miles) per hour, but that seems to be more suggestion than law.

Vehicle after vehicle sped past us in frustration, honking, and gesturing (not so kindly) as we traveled at a paltry pace just over the speed limit. Towing a trailer behind our truck with a total length of 14 meters (47 feet)—on a giant freeway with vehicles merging, exiting, and darting in and out of lanes at high speed—was unnerving.

Watching Michael navigate the traffic was unlike anything I've ever witnessed. I sat quietly, muscles tight, gripping the door handle and braking the air on my side of the truck as cars zipped in and out of the lane as though we weren't there. Michael's hands gripped the wheel, yet he remained stoic and eerily calm. When I asked him about it later that night, he shrugged it off, saying it was like driving the firetruck on a call.

Anaheim, the home of Disneyland, and one of my favorite places in the world, is situated just off I-5. The closer we came to the happiest place in the world, the slower the traffic became. And then it happened; we came to a complete stop and then proceeded to limp slowly through three hours of rush-hour traffic. After days of driving, we found ourselves stuck in sixteen lanes during the worst possible time. This was not fun. And it was a stark reminder of what we had avoided along the way.

We arrived in Chula Vista late in the evening. We were aware this was the eve of doing something we had never done before, and we couldn't wait. We turned in at 9:00 p.m., as we wanted to get to the border crossing checkpoint early. That night, I went to bed giddy with excitement, a joyful heart, and anticipation of what was to come in the morning and over the next six months.

I woke to birds singing. My absolute favorite time of day is early dawn, before the sunrise, and before the stirring of a new day.

Tiptoeing from the bedroom into the kitchen to make a high-test tea and toast, I sat in the quietness of the moment, careful not to wake anyone; it all felt surreal. Ten minutes later, though, the Postage Stamp came alive. The quiet moment had passed between Mia Mukluks' joyful morning barks and Grumpy Tequila's meowing for his treats, but not without the acknowledgment and gratitude for the big, beautiful adventure we were about to undertake.

As we readied the Stamp, we double-checked everything. Driving in Mexico was unfamiliar territory, but we were ready. Based on the timing and information we gathered, the San Ysidro border crossing at the edge of Tijuana appeared the fastest and most direct route for us to drive to Site Number Six. We later learned this border point is the fourth busiest crossing in the world, with both vehicle and foot traffic operating twenty-four hours a day.

Although we knew there were other crossings nearby, we decided we'd enter Mexico at the Tijuana border in the very early morning hours. This entrance was the most accessible to the Mexican Federal Highway 1, also known as the Carretera Transpeninsular Highway—or, simply, Mex 1—that runs 1,711 kilometers (1,063 miles) from Tijuana to Cabo San Lucas. The sun was barely over the horizon when we left the RV park. Determined to avoid the morning rush, we headed straight for the border. Rush hour in this part of California starts even before 6:00 a.m. By 7:00 in the morning, all lanes were crawling.

With each passing mile, our excitement intensified. Knowing we were entering uncharted territory, our resolve grew. Bring on the adventure and uncertainty! We had two stops to make before leaving the States: food and fuel. Luckily, we spotted a Walmart nearby and a gas station across the street. We needed to restock our snacks. *Epic road trips need epic snacks.* There's nothing worse than being between stops, hungry and thirsty, all because of poor planning.

In the store, I searched for mildly nutritious snacks and treats but I discovered new snacks I'd never seen before. Spicy dill pickle chips, chocolate bars, and flavors of jujubes not available in Canada called out to me. Of course, I needed to balance out the chips, chocolate, and jujubes with the healthier choices of trail mix and fresh produce. The avocados, strawberries, and blackberries created a perfect food triangle. I patted myself on the back for thinking ahead and knowing it was all about the balance. The need to have a variety of food on hand was not an indulgence but rather the act of an experienced road warrior. Or so I told myself.

I knew traveling from Canada into the United States carrying fresh produce is almost always a no-no, but I couldn't find any information about bringing in fruits and vegetables into Mexico. I casually asked the checkout person if I could bring avocados across the border. A gentleman in line behind us overheard my question and started hysterically laughing.

He said, "You can bring anything you want into Mexico."

We would learn later that isn't true, but at the moment, I thanked him. As I finished packing up my must-haves for the trip, including my avocados, he turned to me and said,

"But never drive at night."

"*Gracias, Señor*, for your advice," I told him, ready to practice my Spanish voice. Back in the truck, we returned our attention to the route to get us to—and past—the border.

Moving Is Good. Stationary Is Bad.

*T*here it was. The sign: Tijuana, straight ahead! Soon we were in lanes of traffic, all crossing the border. Amazingly, the flow continued to move at a steady pace. Michael's favorite driving statement is "moving is good; stationary is bad." We'd prepared to wait, but the way traffic was advancing, we felt confident we could cross in less than two hours.

No amount of reading, videos, or even talking to others can prepare you for the Tijuana border crossing; it's chaotic yet efficient, with traffic merging indiscriminately and, at times, precariously; it can feel like an accident waiting to happen.

Standard passenger cars and trucks fit nicely into each lane. With our truck and the Postage Stamp, we weren't traditional; we took up a considerable amount of real estate. I felt I could reach out and touch the other vehicles next to us, and I muttered under my breath for them to *pick a lane … but not ours.* Occasionally, Michael would say, "Pardon me?" To which I would reply, "Sorry, I'm just talking to myself."

Suddenly, traffic stood still, so we, along with all the other vehicles, were now stationary. Almost two more hours passed before we reached the actual border. This was our first test of managing our expectations. There's a Spanish saying about time. *"Con el tiempo, todo se consigue."* Loosely translated it means "everything happens in due time." And as such, we finally reached the guardhouse.

It was just after 2:00 p.m. Finally, it was our turn. The guard summoned us with a simple wave of his hand to come forward. As delighted as I was, I became hyper-aware we were about to cross into Mexico.

We approached the guard's booth. In my peripheral vision, to the right of us, just beyond the booth and on the Mexican side of the border, was a truckload of military personnel with assault rifles. Their faces were covered to conceal their identity and they stood at the ready. The sight of them was off-putting, reminding me we were crossing yet another border, this time into Mexico. They had been there all along, but not visible to me until the guard summoned us forward.

You can't unsee these guns. I felt panic rising. I had nothing to hide and was doing nothing wrong, but rifles have never sat well with me. It's not like I'd never seen them before but there were so many. I mentally ran through everything we were bringing into the country. *What if avocados are a no-no? What if….* It's funny how borders bring on a case of the nerves.

Of course, I could feel a hot flash coming on at that most inopportune moment. The beads of sweat were not only forming; they had united to create a raging river, and it was pouring down my back. For the love of all that is holy, this was not helping. I also wasn't accustomed to the humidity of Southern California and Tijuana, and no amount of water was quenching my thirst. Perhaps my excessive perspiration was uncomfortable for the guard because he took one look at me after speaking with Michael and sent us to the next guard. Thank goodness his English was good.

After that, though, Google Translate became our go-to app. We managed to muddle through navigating conversations with hand gestures and a mix of broken Spanish and English. The second guard sent us to the commercial x-ray machine. It's quite a process and very daunting.

First, everyone must exit the cab while the vehicles are being x-rayed. We stood outside on the sidewalk—Grumpy Tequila, Mia Mukluks, and the Two Traveling Fools—waiting in the afternoon heat. Thirty minutes later, we received the thumbs up to move on.

All that remained was for us to get our FMM cards that are required for all who enter Mexico. FMM cards are valid for up to 180 days. After that, visitors must exit Mexico. They are usually called tourist visas and are issued by Mexico's Instituto Nacional de Migración (the INM).

FMM cards in hand, off we went. Getting out of Tijuana and to Ensenada was our top priority. It was now 3:30 p.m., and we were officially in Baja, California, the northern-most state of the Baja Peninsula.

This was it: *la bueno vida—the good life!*

~ॐ~

Eye-opener

*T*he next thing we knew, we were driving through Tijuana, and let me tell you, Tijuana is an eye-opener and not for the faint of heart, especially when towing anything. The streets are tight, and the traffic is crazy. And as we drove on, leaving behind the manicured and well-kept highways and interstates of Canada and the States, we both felt like we were in the Wild West.

Watching Michael navigate the Postage Stamp from my view in the passenger seat through Tijuana's narrow, busy streets, was terrifying; I felt my foot braking an imaginary pedal on my side several times. We plotted our course and headed due south. From this point on, we got very comfortable being uncomfortable. The map becomes interesting and lacks even some of the most basic details. We quickly discovered finding detailed maps was difficult, if not impossible.

Every map we found listed the larger towns only, without noting gas stations, hotels, RV parks, or other amenities one needs when driving long haul. Trusting our instincts and knowing we had done our research did create a sense of unknowing calm, or perhaps our endorphins were keeping the *what-ifs* and *buts* at bay; either way, there was an eerie and yet exciting tension in the truck's cab.

We put some mileage between Tijuana and us. Our goal was to locate an RV park outside Ensenada called La Jolla Beach Camp in Punta Banda. The park seemed like the perfect place for our first night in Mexico. To get to La Jolla, it was a quick jaunt off Mex 1 through some seaside towns. The roads became exceptionally narrow but could accommodate us unless there was oncoming traffic. Our GPS system led us straight to the park, a pleasant surprise as we would come to learn and also very rare; the location was perfect.

This was our first time seeing a different, more authentic side of Mexico. There were no five-star resorts or even three-star hotels. Instead, we saw community—people sitting roadside, sharing conversations at local *taquerias* and vegetable stands. We also saw cows and burros taking themselves for walks. It was an experience like no other. We were in Mexico—real Mexico—and it was all exactly as it should be.

We arrived at the Beach Camp shortly after 4:30 in the afternoon. We were about to get initiated into the new way of accessing the tightest of places, adapting to what was versus what we knew, and cautiously plugging in. The challenge was the steep grade and the power lines above. Again, Michael saved the day and, after some finagling, entered the park with our side mirrors pulled in.

La Jolla did not disappoint. The views of the Pacific Ocean were spectacular—for as far as the eye could see, the beach carried on. We parked in our assigned location on the beach, and for a minute, sat in silence, watching the waves lap the shore as if to say welcome.

RV camping in Mexico is rustic. The experience is mostly no-frills, but who needs them when you can camp on the beach? Since we arrived early in the season, the park was mostly empty except for two other couples off in the distance.

An hour later, while setting up for the night, we got our first introduction to the meaning of "full hookup" in Mexico. Mostly, full hookup here means limited electricity and no potable water—you need to carry in filtered water.

Most RV parks in Mexico supply 30-amp rather than 50-amp electrical service. We found that most parks lacked some electrical component or another during our trek to Site Number Six. Some parks had no electricity at all, only a place to park.

With 50 amps flowing through a 110-volt circuit, you can run pretty much everything as you would in your home, but when there is only 30 amps flowing through that same 110-volt circuit, something has to be unplugged. Lower amperage will restrict the use of multiple appliances—no kettle and toaster at the same time, or the breaker trips. Many RV parks in Mexico offer 110-volt service but with only 30-amp flow, so you must supply your own adapters.

It is important to note that electricity in Mexico is, as they say, juicy. That means the currents change; surge protectors are a must. Juicy also means extension cords get hot to touch and can even melt. We found out that setting up was like putting together a puzzle, inserting the correct adapter into the next, and so on. But watch out: if you use the wrong adapter, things can blow!

After settling in, it was time to celebrate with a walk on the beach. Here we were, at last. We took our first long walk on Mexican soil, which was picture perfect. We both marveled at how far we had come in only three days. Watching the sunset in the Pacific Ocean that evening is a moment I will never forget.

Emotion moved us, and we realized we were no longer talking about this; we were doing it. I questioned how that little girl who dreamed of big, epic adventures got here. *How was this possible?* My eyes leaked a little with gratitude. How could they not?

As we sat watching the sunset, Mia Mukluks entertained us with her crazy antics, running in circles up and down the beach as though she was free at last. It was the stuff of dreams.

_elle,

The Lorax

*W*e rose before the sun and began readying for the day of adventure. Within minutes, the sky filled with burnt orange and pinks like a painting reflecting off the Pacific Ocean.

Our destination, Guerrero Negro, was approximately ten hours away; a few extra minutes of standing in gratitude as the sun launched a new day would be well worth it. Hand in hand, we stood, not wanting to miss a second of what was playing out before us. Soon every rooster, dog, and insect seemed to create a symphony as the sun crested the horizon; a new day had begun.

Our first stop was to fill the truck and our four portable jerry cans with gas; nothing could stop us now. Or so we thought. Back on Mex 1, the roadway runs primarily inland. The desertscape—new to us both—is expansive and stretches for miles. Giant cacti and boulders flanked the narrow road. I had never seen so many!

Along the road, there were many unusual and whimsical looking varieties. Two hours in, we started naming them. The Dr. Seuss cactuses were my favorite. They resembled the Truffula trees in his children's book, *The Lorax*. These are the species, *Fouquieria columnaris*, known in English as Boojum trees. They grow slowly, and then taper off dramatically at the top, causing the tip to droop to one side. Although its appearance is funny-looking, their trunk and branches are made of thorny needles.

Then there are what we called the Mammoths, since they are similar to the California Redwood trees. These giant cacti are enormous, or, as they say in Mexico, *muy grande*. They grow up to 20 meters (65 feet) tall and can weigh more than 10 tons (20,000 pounds). They can live for 300 years and are truly mammoth in every way. Their Latin name is *Pachycereus pringlei* and they are known to many as elephant cactus. In Mexico, they are called *cardón*s, a name derived from the Spanish word *cardo*, meaning thistle. They stand majestic in the arid landscape. They are both foreboding and auspicious at the same time.

There were others along the way, but these two stood out for me as symbols of resilience and adaptation. The scenery remained the same as we continued the windy, narrow road to Guerrero Negro.

It wasn't long before we encountered our first of five military inspection stops—checkpoints placed strategically in the middle of nowhere—which I guess is the point—to deter crime. Although we expected to encounter checkpoints, the first time through one was intimidating. Young soldiers dressed in camouflage head to toe, with their faces partially covered, can leave even the most seasoned traveler a little uneasy. Approaching soldiers who are at the ready with large guns in hand is daunting, especially when traveling as a foreigner in a country where good relationships with the citizens is essential.

Unlike any other interactions we've ever had in Mexico, there are no pleasantries exchanged and, most notably, *no smiles*. Their job is to protect tourists and deter crime; they take the role seriously, as they should. The first checkpoint reinforced everything we'd read about. The questioning lasted about five minutes and they sent us on our way. Our conversation went something like this:

"Where are you from?"

"Canada"

"Where are you going?"

"Los Barriles."

"Why are you going there?"

"To get away from the cold."

"How long?"

"A few months."

"Are you retired?"

"Yes, I am a retired firefighter."

"Oh, *bombero*. Advance."

Translation: *Oh, fireman*. And just like that, we were on our way. Being a retired *bombero* in Mexico has its privileges, we discovered.

Smiling again, we continued onward to Guerrero Negro. We continuously referred to our paper map, which was now tearing at the seams and lacking most of the essential details. Yet it provided an overall sense of where we were going in the way only a physical map can. We knew getting to Guerrero Negro meant crisscrossing the peninsula and climbing numerous mountain passes. We hadn't ascended the first mountain pass but we could see it ahead in the distance, and I was looking forward to the climb and view.

The world with all its bigness can be so small. The same mountain range, the American Cordillera, extends from Canada through Mexico, and we'd traverse sections of them a few times on our trip. Soon, we'd cross over the Sierra de Juárez and Sierra de San Pedro Mártir ranges.

We would also navigate the Sierra de la Giganta mountain passes through to the Catavina boulder fields. Coming across them, I felt the boulders seemed strangely out of place. To me, they were like ginormous marbles that had been placed strategically in the fields by ancient goliaths. I thought about the health problems we had overcome, and what we still had to deal with. Somehow, those big marbles helped me find peace with it all.

The Hare

$\mathcal{W}$e'd driven for hours, and Mia Mukluks was beginning to stir in her crate; she needed a walk, and we all needed a break except for Grumpy Tequila, whose love of travel was evident in his many sleeping poses for hours on end.

Unlike the beautiful rest stops in America, there are none on Mex 1, so finding a safe place to pull over is a challenge. We lucked out as we rounded a corner onto a long straightaway. There it was, the perfect place to pull over. There was even a prominent shoulder. It felt a little like divine intervention.

We eased off the road and came to a stop. Mia Mukluks was in full performance mode in her crate, turning circles of joy. We exited the truck, and the midday heat filled our lungs. It was dry, without a breeze, yet refreshing as we walked around to the trailer. What surprised me most, though, was how peaceful it was.

There is a beautiful, harsh serenity in the desert. Before traveling, I thought the desert to be mostly lifeless and barren. But that's not true at all. The desert is a diverse ecosystem constantly adapting to survive and thrive in the most challenging conditions.

A couple of small lizards scurried by as we sat outside. Perhaps, Michael joked, they were casing us out to see what deliciousness we'd offer. Birds flew overhead, swooping down to check us all out; maybe Michael was right. When I stood to grab a drink from the truck's cab, I saw something move out of the corner of my eye. My first thought was a rattlesnake. I have no fear of snakes, but I want nothing to do with those who can hurt me. It was no rattlesnake. It was a black-tailed jack rabbit. Actually, they aren't rabbits; they are hares.

Clearly, I was in need of new glasses.

Black-tailed hares have the most laughable, outlandish ears that serve an essential purpose: to keep them cool. And as if the ears didn't make this hare odd enough looking, its hind legs are oversized, making it look like it's wearing clown shoes. But nature and evolution are ingenious and constantly adapting for survival. These odd legs lend themselves to epic speeds of up to 48 kilometers (30 miles) an hour and leaps 6 meters (20 feet) high in the air.

I wanted to capture the moment. I reached cautiously for my camera, but it was not to be. My movement created tension, and just like that—with a leap, a zig, and zag, the hare dashed into the desert.

We saw so many creatures in those few minutes, but where did they get their water? There was none in sight: *nada*, zilch, zip. And yet, plants were growing, flowers were blooming, and clearly, life existed. After our short, but much-needed break, we continued. A much steeper pass lay straight ahead.

At first, the ascent was gradual but the grade increased with each corner we rounded; even the truck protested as it labored up the mountain. As we crawled up the pass, our three-quarter-ton truck slowed, dropping from sixth gear to second.

Taking advantage of the slower pace, I grabbed my camera and started capturing pictures of the beauty and vastness. It's in these moments I realize how small we are. Earth is in a constant state of reinvention, despite humans.

As we climbed—what I was now calling the corkscrew—we saw no summit in sight. With each blind corner we rounded, I thought, *this must be the top*, but it was simply another blind corner. Higher and higher we went.

We were both happy to have this stretch of the road to ourselves. We noted the many crosses and monuments marking those who hadn't been so fortunate. This was a treacherous and deadly section of the road, with a rockface to our right and a sheer drop-off on the other side of the road. And no guardrail.

As we rounded another corner, barreling toward us and partially in our lane, was a large commercial tractor-trailer. Amazingly, neither of us lost our side mirrors, which seemed inevitable. It was much too close though, and reminded us of the reality of the driving dangers.

Michael has a saying, "If it doesn't scare you, you won't gain any confidence." Sure, but truthfully, I wasn't looking for more confidence!

We decided it was time to readjust our expectations of the highways. Serendipitously, "Let It Ride" by Bachman-Turner Overdrive began playing on the radio. We laughed and decided it was a sign.

The Gap

*W*e pulled over to regroup and fill the tank with the last of the jerry cans we filled in El Rosario. Towing even the tiniest of homes over mountain passes burns fuel, lots of it. Unbeknownst to us, we were about to learn our next memorable lesson.

Locating gas stations is difficult on this stretch of Mex 1. On top of that, not all gas stations can accommodate trailers and the radius required to turn them. Even the most determined and seasoned RV travelers pause before entering a gas station. After a while, you know what fits and what doesn't.

We welcomed each brief break to stretch our legs and search for more road trips essentials—code for cool treats. As we pulled into the parking lot, we discovered a little taqueria that offered Mexico's finest *tamales* and *Agua de Jamaica,* a delicious cold beverage.

Tamales are my favorite eat-on-the run food; perfect little parcels wrapped in corn husks and tied neatly in a bow. Tamales are a traditional Mexican dish, made with a corn-based dough called *masa* and filled with various meats, beans, cheese, and potatoes. They are a must-try. The corn husk envelopes the dough and filling, which are removed and discarded once the filling has cooked.

Agua de Jamaica is made with dried Roselle Hibiscus flowers, hot water, and sugar to taste. Steeped to perfection to concoct a refreshing caffeine-free tea, it's served over ice and tastes similar to cranberry juice, but slightly less tart and with a hint of lime. I call it Mexico's version of iced tea. Although not specifically unique to Mexico, almost all Latin countries offer this refreshing and beautifully colorful drink.

While we ate our tamales and sipped our "iced tea," we studied our limited paper map again to ensure we were on track. From what we could ascertain, Guerrero Negro, our stop for the night, was approximately four-and-a-half-hours away, requiring us to refuel at least once more. No problem, right?

Aside from the close call on the pass, everything went according to plan. Having used the last fuel in the jerry cans, we decided we'd refuel in the next town. *The only problem is the gas station had shut down two years earlier.* According to the locals, we could find gas in the next town. But there was no gas station when we got to the next town either. Meanwhile, the gas gauge continued to drop and there was no more fuel in the jerry cans. We both felt nervous. There's no road side assistance in Mexico … and the cows and burros don't accept credit cards.

We didn't know about the "Gas Gap" that existed between El Rosario and Guerrero Negro, a stretch of more than 360 kilometers (200 miles). We drove on, telling ourselves the next town would undoubtedly have gas. Wrong. Shortly after passing through the last village, we passed an elderly gentleman sitting roadside with a sign that read, "*Gasolina.*"

We thought it odd and carried on for another twenty minutes. And then it happened. The dreaded fuel light lit up, indicating we'd soon be running on fumes. We'd be out of gas; we were in the middle of nowhere and we had no choice but to turn around. I'm sure you've heard of a three-point-turn; with the tiny home in tow, we were a thirty-point turn. Back we went to the Gasolina man, who, thankfully, had remained at his post. As he waved us into his makeshift gas station, I wondered how many times this happened in a day.

As we pulled up, he looked up and smiled at us with a big toothless smile that said, "I got you." After exchanging pleasantries through broken English and Spanish, we discovered it was good we turned back, as there were no gas stations ahead for a couple of hours.

Jose Luis told us he could help and pulled out his impressive tools. A stick with notches carved in it, a garden hose, and a pen and paper. The process, albeit archaic, was efficient and accurate. Jose Luis inserted the stick into his 170-liter (45-gallon) drum of gasoline, pulling it out to show us where the gas left a marking on the measuring stick.

According to his trusty stick, the drum held about 125 liters (33 gallons). Jose Luis began readying to fill our tank by inserting one end of the hose into the drum and the other into his mouth to siphon the gas from the barrel by sucking it into the hose. And from there into our truck's tank.

About fifteen minutes later, he removed the hose, measured the gas in his drum again using the trusty notched stick, and showed us what remained. He then took out his pen and paper and did the calculations. We purchased 121 liters (32 gallons) of gasoline, almost draining the rest of his drum, giving us more than enough to get us to the next gas station.

Thank goodness for Jose Luis and his Gasolina sign. We learned later that night that El Rosario is the last fuel stop heading south before entering the Gas Gap.

We were approaching Guerrero Negro two hours later, with our valuable and memorable lesson on our minds. That, and our gratitude for the ingenuity and creativity of Jose Luis, the kind Gasolina rescuer.

Sparks in the Night

*W*e pulled into Guerrero Negro at dusk, later than expected but a little wiser and more schooled on traveling the roads in Baja. It was time to relax, so we treated ourselves to dinner. There was a local restaurant in the RV park.

For our setup routine of the Postage Stamp, Michael takes the outside and I take the inside; it feels a little like pink and blue jobs, and I guess it is, as I know nothing about sewage hookup and the like. But I'm so grateful Michael does! We have our respective jobs. And, truth be told, mine is more pleasant and less stinky.

My tasks are to ready the inside for relaxation and make sure nothing has shifted during our travels. Opening each cupboard with caution, I take a step back, just in case anything wants to spring out at me. If you've ever opened a cupboard door and had a three-pound tub of white sugar launch itself at you—first onto the counter, followed by a bounce off the stainless-steel sink, then landing on the floor narrowly missing your foot and ending with a loud thud—you'll know exactly why.

Luckily, everything was mostly in place and today there were no flying sugar tubs or anything else on the attack. In the early evening, RV parks become a beehive of activity as more and more travelers arrive for the night. An older model, light blue motorhome pulled up alongside us, and soon, the driver was also outside setting up for the evening.

Pop, pop, pop! *What the hell was that?* The motorhome beside us started to smoke at the electrical connection. Sparks and pops continued from the box. Michael was on the opposite side of our trailer, hooking up the water. When he heard the *pop, pop, pop,* he dropped the hose and ran full speed toward the electrical box. By the time he got to the pole, our neighbor had already detached their connection. Michael, too, pulled the plug to our hookup, and we all stood watching, shaking our heads as the box continued smoking.

Smoking motorhomes, junction boxes, loud pops, and flying sparks are never good signs on road trips. Nowhere in any RV literature does it say what to do in the case of juicy electricity or sparks and smoking connections.

Upon further inspection, they determined the electrical arcing had damaged the circuit board beyond repair. Worse, the power surge had blown the motorhome's inverter. Inverters are critical to converting DC power to AC power; RV systems use inverters to enable the battery to run air conditioning and appliances. Finding an inverter was going to be a significant challenge. And although this was frightening, it could have been much worse. The motorhome could have caught fire.

We wouldn't be hooking up to the power here again. Instead, Michael, ever the firefighter, plugged in an extension cord and ran it from our trailer's internal battery to provide light for our neighbor. During dinner that night, we learned from another traveler that the RV park had been rewired that day and was having considerable problems; *uh, no kidding.*

This little fiasco did give us the opportunity to meet our now-neighborly motorhome driver, John, who told us he was returning from Loreto to Canada for the winter and would have the motorhome repaired there. He laughed as he stated, "It's thirty-four years old and it owes me nothing." John told us in Mexico, you learn to take things in stride. This would be an important lesson and one we would remember.

We met others that night; all except John were heading south. As we laughed and shared our tales of the day, nearly all relating to driving

Mex 1, we discovered the majority were, like us, on their maiden voyage. It seemed things were only going to get more interesting.

When we returned from dinner to the Stamp, we discovered we weren't unscathed by the smoking electrical issues. We attempted to turn on the lights and—nothing. The arcing had burned out two fuses. But this was only a minor inconvenience, thank goodness.

John, like us, was an early riser, and he had a long day ahead of him—his goal was the U.S. border. We bid *hasta la vista* to John and wished him safe travels back to Edmonton for the winter. Later, I wondered why John was returning to Canada for the winter, the coldest time of the year, but I forgot to ask in the commotion of sparks and blown fuses.

We, too, had a long day ahead. Our goal was Los Barriles. The night before, several campers told us it was impossible to make it there in one day, as it was an eleven-hour-long drive, for sure. We agreed to evaluate along the way as needed.

With the sparks behind us and new friends made, we headed out in the morning, energized and ready for whatever came next.

Too Close for Comfort

*W*e left Guerrero Negro feeling confident. Nothing could stop us now. Here we were, two Canadians driving through Mexico in style. We weren't aiming to be ostentatious, rather just the opposite, but it's difficult, if not impossible, to blend in with the Stamp and a very large, shiny new truck. Every time we pulled into a *pueblo*, the locals waved and gave us thumbs up; the sheer length of our caravan seemed to shock many. Mexican men loved Michael's truck.

The retired firefighter stickers Michael proudly displayed on truck windows seemed to evoke reverence and respect for us, too. On seeing the decals, conversations would often ensue and we met many volunteer *bomberos*. Just as in Canada and the United States, this camaraderie transcends borders and language.

It wasn't long before we encountered our next military checkpoint. Even though we had already experienced our first stop, it was still intimidating. Again, no pleasantries were exchanged and no smiles showed until they saw Mia Mukluks and wanted to pet her, who was happy to oblige. These young men are in high-risk situations daily. To see them laugh and talk to Mia warmed my heart.

And, just like that, we were back on our way, driving through unique scenery, like nothing I have ever seen before. The Baja California Peninsula extends some 1,220 kilometers (760 miles) in length. But it only stretches about 320 kilometers (199 miles) at its widest point. The contrast between the turquoise blue waters of the Sea of Cortez and the Pacific Ocean, with the quiet, rocky desert and its various ecosystems is magical and breathtaking. The further we drove into the desert, the more cacti and succulent plants we saw growing in the most hostile environment, again a reminder to me of their perfect resilience and perseverance.

From time to time, we slowed down or stopped so I could snap pictures, but the images were lacking; they couldn't do justice to what I was seeing. Standing beside an elephant cactus reminded me of how insignificant we humans are in the world. Each region we drove through was new and magical. The mountain passes were significantly higher than I expected, with views of desert valleys for miles.

As we relaxed into the drive, we laughed about the night before and shared how lucky we were that all we had lost were two fuses. Although this meant replacing them, it was a small price to pay for juicy electricity, which we were beginning to understand happens often.

Fortunately, we had gained an hour once we crossed into the southern peninsula state of Baja California Sur, and we needed the extra daylight. As we had already learned, the predicted time means nothing; it's merely an estimate.

Our next stop would be Santa Rosalía. This small seaside town intrigued me and its history was fascinating. I grew up in Hedley, a small mining village in British Columbia about four hours east of Vancouver. Hedley ran a former gold and nickel mine in its glory days. Santa Rosalía had a familiar story of boom and bust. The town was only a couple of hours away, so it was an easy drive and a nice place to top up the tank.

With each passing mile, we noticed the landscape was again changing. We were about to enter the El Vizcaíno Biosphere Reserve, centrally located on the Baja peninsula in the Sebastian Volcano region between the Gulf of Mexico and the Pacific Ocean.

We learned that the biosphere is a sanctuary for grey whales, who often frequent the bays, along with sea lions, and dolphins. And flora and fauna of the reserve are endemic to the region; unlike the arid deserts we'd driven through, this landscape is teeming with life. Although we didn't get to see any ourselves, many people told us they spotted bighorn sheep and mule deer, and some were lucky enough to see the disappearing pronghorn antelopes, survivors from a distant world.

Other travelers told us that history is written in the fossil beds and on the walls through petroglyphs. These wonders we would need to explore in the future. We were in awe as we drove through the biosphere and the volcanic complex called Tres Vírgenes with its three volcanoes: El Viejo, the oldest, El Azufre, and the youngest, El Vírgen.

Before we knew it, we were again climbing another mountain pass. It's funny how I thought the ascent was so steep the day before, yet now, comparatively, that slope seemed so gentle. We went up and up again; the grade was at least thirty percent steep in places and the truck geared down, slowing us to a snail's pace. Round and round we went up the corkscrew.

And then, there it was: the cerulean blue of the Sea of Cortez. We reached the summit after a final hairpin corner and we were awestruck. The view created such an intense wave of gratitude and joy—we were both speechless.

The Sea of Cortez, glistening and breathtaking, is a sapphire that captures your heart. It seems endless and magical. There are no words to describe its beauty adequately. Down, down, down we slowly descended the mountain, into Santa Rosalia, each turn leading to another as though we were riding a giant, twisting rollercoaster. I was instantly in love and enchanted.

During the descent, the Sea of Cortez on our left was juxtaposed by the large modern mining operation, El Boleo, or The Ball. Here, workers mine copper, cobalt, zinc, and manganese deposits. Not unlike other mines, El Boleo has a tumultuous past and the mine is what put Santa Rosalía on the map. In the late 1800s, it became one of the world's largest producing copper mines. Over the years, France, Mexico, Canada, and Korea have operated El Boleo. Its history is as colorful as the town itself.

We fully came down from our ascent, staying on Mex 1 all the way, bringing us directly into the bustling port of Santa Rosalía. At first glance, the town is both beautiful and harsh; industrial yet inviting. The imposing skeleton of rusted and twisted steel stands in stark contrast to the translucent blue sea. We rolled down all the windows. I immediately tasted the salty ocean air, which felt like it was permeating every cell in my body.

The Patina of Santa Rosalía

*P*erhaps an homage to its past glory days, the influence in Santa Rosalía is French, with a touch of the Wild West, with wooden structures and colorful designs lining the cobblestone streets.

Unlike other seaside towns in Mexico, Santa Rosalía does not offer endless miles of sandy shoreline. In fact, it's quite the opposite. The shoreline is rocky, gritty, and rugged, yet stunning. Something revealing—yet hidden—sets Santa Rosalía apart from other Baja communities but I can't place my finger on it. Perhaps it's the French influence or the ties to Canada. I sensed something oddly familiar. Maybe it was the mine itself, reminding me of my childhood playground in Canada. There was something about Santa Rosalía that made me yearn to know more.

Visitors are drawn into the town center with a large and colorful sign welcoming all. Each letter features a picture depicting historical stories. There is a Malecon, or *esplanade*, that beckons all who come to walk and sit to take in the view of the spectacular Sea of Cortez.

Rich in history, Santa Rosalía is home to Iglesia de Santa Bárbara, a magnificent church of steel, stained glass windows, and stamped metal. The church is rumored to have been designed by the famous French Civil engineer Alexandra-Gustave Eiffel—yes, the same designer of the Eiffel Tower. Inside, the homage to the Eiffel tower is clear.

We discovered a lovely pastry shop, Panadería El Boleo, offering French and Mexican pastries alike, that's been in business since 1901. The shop, to this day, still uses wood ovens to bake their delectable treats! Further on, we found the Romo Store Café for coffee and tea. Back to the Malecon we went for a lazy stroll.

We sat gazing at the sea, feasting on our pastries, me sipping tea and Michael relishing every drop of his coffee, while Mia Mukluks lay sleepily at my feet. I felt as though I was in a whimsical seaside fantasy, as if an artist had captured us picnicking on the bench.

I will forever cherish that moment. We savored every morsel and I ran my finger along the inside of the bag, ensuring not a single bit of deliciousness was missed. An hour had passed, yet we felt as though we had just sat down. We vowed to make this a ritual on every road trip. And we have.

We were both richer, having experienced that moment, but now it was time to get back on the journey. We went hand in hand, searching for a hardware store for fuses. Fuses for RVs can be tough to find, but we were hopeful, and we found a hardware store with plenty in stock only two blocks away.

Michael replaced the fuses, and we began our next leg of the journey. Having escaped any of the catastrophes and hazards we had heard tales of, we were starting to become very comfortable, maybe too comfortable.

We exited Santa Rosalía on the long winding hill; the competing contrasts of the Sea of Cortez on one side and copper hills on the opposite made me wonder what the early settlers must have thought when they arrived from France. At that moment, I understood how easy it was for people to fall in love with Baja and never want to leave.

Little did we know that some of the best vistas were only minutes down the road. And again, as we drove on wonderstruck, we both started to question how it could get any better, just as we had only a few days earlier driving the coastal highway in Oregon. *Seriously, how much better could it possibly get?*

With lots of fuel and daylight hours ahead of us, we continued our mission to get to Site Number Six. The highway hugged the coastline for the first thirty minutes after leaving Santa Rosalía; every turn offered beautiful vistas, each breathtaking and unique. Neither of us had expected the visceral effect of the scenery.

Then, the road turns inward at San Bruno, a small *pueblo*, and we were back in the desert. The landscape changed from sand and sea to boulders and majestic cactus. The cool ocean breezes were now behind us.

With each passing mile, the temperature climbed higher and higher. It wasn't long before we saw the first mirage in the distance; shimmering water on the hot pavement. Soon, we came upon mirage after mirage. Each one drew us in, inviting and offering refuge from the heat but only to disappear as we neared. Flashbacks to my youth of hot summer days flooded my mind. In the southern Okanagan, where summers are dry and humidity is almost nonexistent, my family, friends, and I spent any waking moments we could in the river.

As we bantered about the remaining leg of the journey, my excitement grew. According to our limited information, Mulegé was about thirty minutes away. We needed to refuel the truck, have a quick stretch, walk Mia Mukluks, and check on the best traveler ever, Grumpy Tequila. We rounded a corner, and then straight ahead, I saw palm trees. This was no mirage; this was Mulegé. Having just left the desert, it was like being parachuted into a tropical lushness.

Palm and mangrove trees line the Rio Mulegé, a rare desert river. What appears to be a sleepy little village features a grand and inviting entrance which leads you to the town center, where the local artisans display their wares.

After a quick tour and refueling, we took in the Misión Santa Rosalía de Mulegé. We had limited time but the mission seemed like a must-do. It did not disappoint. Standing atop a rocky outcrop, the mission's simplicity and size make a statement, and, as missions go, this one is worth exploring. Jesuit father Juan Manuel de Basaldúa founded the mission in 1705. Construction was under the supervision of Father Francisco Escalante and finally completed in 1766, using only local stone. The mission still stands today, offering a glimpse into the past. The grounds offer various panoramic vistas to enjoy. With 360-degree views, the founders certainly maximized the breathtaking surroundings.

What was to be a brief stop turned into one hour and it was worth every minute. That's the thing about road trips; the destination is the journey. Back on the road, and still amazed at what we had accidentally discovered, we add Mulegé to our must-visit list further on future drives. As we left the town heading south, we vowed to return. There was much more to discover and experience in this hidden gem.

Within twenty minutes of leaving Mulegé, we saw the most beautiful beaches. Mostly untouched, these beaches are the most spectacular of all beaches in Mexico. We had heard about a bay off the Gulf of Mexico where white-sand beaches, coves, inlets, and sparkling waters of the Sea of Cortez speak to anyone who loves the sea and nature.

We were now in Bahía Concepción, a place unlike anything I have ever seen in my life. I warn you, though, if you are a lover of all things untouched, you may get stuck here on purpose; many do. The entire bay is exquisite, heavenly, surreal, and simply magnificent.

There are several *playas*, each beach more beautiful than the last. The shoreline, amid the backdrop of rugged rock formations with protected bays and sparkling turquoise waters, with mile after mile of white sand, left us speechless. We had to stop. This magnificent piece of Baja was not to be passively driven by and stored in the memory banks for a later date. No, we had to stop to admire what was before us to experience. How could we not?

We learned from two other couples, who also had pulled over, that beach camping, *aka* boondocking, is encouraged. The fee for all this beauty is around ten dollars a night, including a *palapa*, a little structure with a thatched roof. Although there are no services to hook up to—no connections to water, electricity, or sewer it's a magical place, and well worth forgoing creature comforts.

I looked longingly at my paddleboard mounted to the roof of the truck. I knew we couldn't take it down today, but soon. And I couldn't wait to explore the bays in the future on my board. Oh, the places we would go!

Our return trip home to Canada in the spring was already filling up with places we needed to stop and explore. Bahía Concepción was added to the ever-growing list.

Car Face

We had at least six more hours of driving time to Los Barriles, and even with the hour we had gained, I was beginning to think perhaps we had been too ambitious. We would need to re-evaluate when we reached La Paz. According to the map, our next place to stop was Loreto, about two hours away. Still, Number Six was getting closer and closer with each passing hour.

The scenery on day five was beginning to blend in—a cactus is a cactus—and the romantic glamour and newness had most definitely worn off. Nothing had changed, but we had spent nearly five days driving eleven to thirteen hours in a truck towing a trailer. These were long days. Even professional truck drivers stop after eight hours of driving. But we were so close.

I felt punchy, and I was feeling off. But why now, after thousands of miles? It wasn't from physical exhaustion; instead, I was feeling impatient. Perhaps this was normal at this point in the trip. But I began to wonder, *had we been impetuous?* I knew we had researched everything we could, but really, *what if?*

Michael remained excited. Perhaps he sensed a change of attitude? If so, he was correct, I started to question my determinedness, and the thought of being so far away from loved ones hit me. It was quiet in the cab; we couldn't pick up any radio stations, so my mind was free to conjure up all sorts of scenarios—and all were causing angst. I told myself it was simply cold feet on this maiden voyage and that many had done this before us.

I think Michael decided to add some brevity to the mood. Out of nowhere, he said, "I have car face."

"Car face?" I asked, laughing so hard I could barely get out the words. I had never heard anyone use this term before. Of course, I hadn't. There was no such saying. Michael explained to me that when you have been driving for so many hours or days, you can't help but get car face.

In some strange way, it made sense. Driving from point A to point B was best known to me as windshield time. And what you did with that time in between either enhanced or made the trip arduous; laughter was good.

Years later, we would laugh about having car face. At that moment, it was the funniest thing I had ever heard Michael say. Every time I looked over at him, I began to laugh hysterically. Mia Mukluks looked on, smiling in her crate; I am sure she wondered what all the laughter was about.

Suddenly a song came on we both liked, and we were both singing at the top of our lungs. Even Mia Mukluks joined in, or maybe she was letting us know our singing left much to be desired. Meanwhile, Grumpy Tequila watched us with grumpy car face.

Thank you, Michael Franti & Spearhead for writing "I'm Alive (Life Sounds Like)." For nearly four minutes, we sang and car-danced. And, just like that, the angst was gone … or at least quieted for the moment. Songs are so powerful; it's amazing how a tune can get in your soul and wake you up.

Yes, we each had car face, but we also had laughter, and we were creating memories, *while we can*, moments that can only come from epic road trips. Between the song, car dance, and laughter, I felt inspired and grateful again.

And then …

We rounded a corner on our assent to see an oncoming semi-truck tilted sideways in our lane, coming straight at us. A smaller utility truck in front of us narrowly missed being hit and crushed by moving as close as he could to the jagged rock face. He barely escaped what could have been an inevitable disaster only seconds before us.

It's funny how time, as we know it, changes in the moments of impending danger and disaster. Only moments before, the road was wide open and safe. We were laughing and carrying on, and now everything was about to change.

As we continued into the turn, the highway seemed to narrow even more—likely an illusion. What wasn't an illusion was there was no way we could both fit in the one lane. That moment stretched on for what seemed like minutes, yet it was probably only five seconds. The impact was imminent, and we all knew it would be catastrophic.

Michael gripped the steering wheel at "10 and 2" and looked straight ahead. His eyes were wide open as though searching for a solution. He told me later he was evaluating any possible scenarios. But there was no place to go. The cliff face and jagged boulders protruding from the mountainside were on the passenger side, and there was no shoulder. So narrow was the road that there wasn't even a white line to indicate the road's edge. The oncoming lane provided even fewer solutions with no guardrail; it would lead to certain death as the drop off the mountainside was inescapable.

I grabbed the passenger door handle and gripped it as hard as possible. There was no way for us to avoid what was about to happen. The trailer of the oncoming semi-truck continued to tip further and would hit the driver's side first, crushing Michael. I was terrified and felt utterly useless. However, this did not stop me from trying to pump the imaginary brakes. The truck trailer would only tear a gaping hole in the Postage Stamp if we were lucky. My only thought was, *please, save Michael.*

Neither of us made a sound. There was no place to go to avoid what was about to happen. We were, as they say, between a rock and a hard place.

And as if God himself had reached down at the moment of impact, the oncoming semi-trailer truck righted itself. Had I not experienced this, I would never have believed the miracle right before our eyes; the trucker was once again fully upright in his lane. He passed so close to us that if Michael's window had been down, he could have reached out and touched the truck.

The look on the trucker's face was sheer terror and disbelief. Thankfully neither driver had overcorrected, creating a chain of events that would have resulted in a horrific crash.

Although we barely skimmed past each other with what felt like less than an inch to spare, we did not touch. How the side mirrors did not catch each other still boggles me. I continued to hold my breath; all we needed was to complete the turn. And as long as the tail end of the Stamp did not clip the other trailer as he completed his turn, we would all be okay. And just like that, we were through—untouched but certainly not unscathed.

It had to have been divine intervention. At the bottom of the mountain, we saw the gentleman driving the utility truck—who had barely evaded a crash himself—pulled over on the side of the road. He exited his cab, raising his hands in the air in prayer. That was the closest we have ever come to death on any road trip, and we have taken many.

We were both shaken to the core but grateful to be alive. That close call reminded us how quickly things could change. It struck me as odd that in the terrifying moment, unlike in the movies, there were no screams, no declarations of undying love, just silent terror and a collective sense of disbelief and shock. It took some time before either of us could form a coherent sentence. I have never been so grateful and ecstatic to reach a summit in my life! That was the first brush, but not the last.

Typically, when Michael expresses his shock, it comes out loud and full of colorful words. But not today. Instead, he spoke quietly and directly.

"Higher Power." That was all he said.

I still had no words.

All the *what-ifs* flooded my mind; *what if we had collided?* The thought made me sick to my stomach. With hands shaking, I sat quietly. Having an accident in Canada was one thing, but having an accident in a country where I could not even speak the language was another thing. We had all the insurance coverages and such, but, *what if???* Insurance doesn't undo death.

We had just experienced the reality of narrow roads and close calls. Thankfully, we received a Hail Mary at the last possible moment.

We carried onto Loreto in silence, with the lingering tension and awareness that life is fatal; we must live fully *while we can*. We both knew how fortunate we were. And we, too, now had our own terrifying road story. One is more than enough; we were far less naïve, having narrowly escaped. We truly understood the danger and hazards of the roads.

We entered Loreto and opted to top up the gas tank and head for La Paz. Exploring was not on our minds and Loreto would have to wait, perhaps until a day when we were fresh and not reeling. We remind ourselves these are the stories you tell later in life and laugh about. But not today; today was too soon and too close for comfort.

Once our nerves were settling down, we settled back into the drive. We were determined to get to Los Barriles; we were both ready to stay the course.

Arriving in La Paz at 4:30 p.m., with at least an hour of daylight to spare, we felt confident. We were told we were less than forty-five minutes away and it would not be dark before 6:00 p.m., leaving us plenty of time.

Getting out of La Paz proved to be challenging. A couple of tropical storms that had hit during the summer had wreaked havoc on the roads. In some sections, there were potholes the size of baby bassinets. The GPS had us going in circles and it was far more challenging to get out of La Paz than we had anticipated. We took a few wrong turns, which added to our time, but we finally found our way out and back on the road to Site Number Six.

The beautiful, simple life. (©Julie Shipman)

The wind beckons. (©Julie Shipman)

The Portuguese man-of-war, beautiful but painful. (©Alicia Campbell/Pixabay)

The majestic Haystack Rock of Cannon Beach, Oregon. (©tmparker228/Pixabay)

Crossing into Mexico. (©Julie Shipman)

"Big Mama!" the mighty cardón cacti, giant of the desert. (©Julie Shipman)

The Neighbors. (©Julie Shipman)

The jumping cholla cactus—don't stand too close! (©Julie Shipman)

A black-tailed hare on alert. (©Pixabay)

The Boojum tree. (©Julie Shipman)

Roselle Hibiscus flowers used to make Agua de Jamaica. (©Robert Lens/Pixabay)

Tres Vírgenes volcanic complex, another wonder to explore. (©Vipersniper/iStock)

Cascada Sol de Mayo Waterfall, Baja California Sur, Mexico. (©Julie Shipman)

The abandoned remains of the El Boleo French Mining Company in Santa Rosalía. (©izanbar/iStock)

La Romana of El Triunfo, known as the smokestack. (©Victor Yee Fotografia/iStock)

Michael kiting. (©Julie Shipman)

Jo in her beloved Los Barriles. (©Julie Shipman)

A Mobula ray jumps out of the water in the Sea of Cortez. (©Gudkov.Andrey/iStock)

Bahía Concepción, the crown jewel of Baja beaches. (©Julie Shipman)

Life and Death are celebrated in Mexico. (©Julie Shipman)

Just GO!

*A*s we pulled onto Mex 1, we heard a familiar sound that causes cringes even in the most seasoned driver: a police siren. Michael slowed to let them pass, but they slowed with us. We pulled over, and they stopped, too. Yikes! Being pulled over is never ideal; being pulled over in a foreign country adds an entirely new dimension to the scene.

Even though I tried to calm myself, my heart was racing, my hands were shaking, and I was sweating. Nothing says "guilty" more than a middle-aged woman profusely sweating and shaking. But guilty of what? Rationally, I knew we had done nothing wrong; *maybe we had been going too slow?*

The two police officers exited their cruiser and approached the truck on the passenger side, due to what I assume was because of the heavy traffic on the driver's side. Still, it felt intimidating as they approached.

I rolled down my window, and the younger police officer began to speak in Spanish. I froze. Michael speaks some Spanish, although he is by no means fluent. I confuse Spanish with French at times, which I also don't speak very well but I can grasp some essential words. Therefore, I often come out talking in a type of Franglish—an odd combination of French, Spanish, and English—meaning I am illiterate and cannot answer even the most basic questions without translating from Spanish to French to English and back. By the time I find an answer, people have moved on.

The young officer, sensing my struggle, proceeded to tell us in broken English we had a burnt-out taillight and that it was dangerous and an infraction to drive like this. He then pulled out his ticket book and handed it to the senior ranking officer behind him.

Through hand gestures and broken English, Michael was instructed to accompany the younger officer to the back of the Postage Stamp and check the taillights. Indeed, the left taillight was burnt out. Once Michael was back in the truck, the officer resumed his stance on having to write a ticket.

Michael addressed the senior officer in his best Spanish, saying, *"Gracias por decírmelo, lo siento."* "Thank you for telling me, I am sorry."

The young officer then turned to his partner, who was looking mostly disinterested but official. They chatted briefly. When they were through, the young officer turned back to us, looking past me and addressing Michael, *"Señor,* you pay a fine of $20 cash and no ticket."

Sadly, this happens in Mexico from time to time; it is a hustle. Locals refer to it as a *mordida,* which translates to "bite." It is essentially a bribe to avoid a ticket. Before leaving, we were made aware of this little scheme and were instructed never to give cash to an officer. But in this instance, our taillight was burnt out, so he was correct in pulling us over. I have heard some people humorously refer to the process as Mexican road tax. We legitimately had a broken taillight so a ticket and fine were in order.

"Cuanto?" Michael asked.

"Veinte dólares," the now-engaged senior officer replied.

I took a $20.00 Canadian bill from my wallet. When I handed it to him, the older officer looked confused. He looked at the twenty and showed it to the young officer. He seemed confused, too.

The older officer asked, "What is this?"

"$20.00 Canadian," I answered.

And with that, the older officer returned the money and told us to "Go!"

Michael wasn't sure he heard him correctly and asked, *"Pardon?"*

The older officer repeated loudly, "Just GO!" This time he pointed in the direction of Los Barriles.

Later, we would learn that it's hard to exchange Canadian currency in Mexico. Perhaps this is a good strategy to avoid future *mordida*. Getting lost and being pulled over took up valuable daylight hours and it was approaching dusk. Still, if Los Barriles was close, we would be there before dark.

Wrong!

We carried on, not realizing that this—our last stretch of the trip— would be by far the most treacherous stretch of Mex 1. The road is a mountain pass and dangerous at the best of times, with drop-offs and blind corners at almost every turn. But this year, to make matters worse, the road was under construction and repair from the hundred-year rains of the summer. Heavy downpours had damaged the highway and washed it out thoroughly in some areas.

My excitement turned to anxiety; we knew driving in the dark was an absolute no. We were about to break our covenant—no driving in the dark! I have never been more acutely aware that we were in over our heads. I knew this hadn't been the right decision. Our anticipation, exhaustion, and enthusiasm outweighed our common sense.

Thirty minutes later, we saw a posted distance sign. The realization we were at least an hour away became clear. There was no place to pull off the road or turn around, and worse, it was now pitch black.

Contrary to stories you may have seen in the media, what makes driving after sunset treacherous is not because of potential *banditos* waiting for you around every corner, because there aren't any. Baja is one of the safest places in Mexico—unless you are driving at night.

Because this is when you might meet a number of animals. Cats, dogs, chickens, cows, goats, and horses roam freely to forage for food at night. To say nothing of the wild burros and other night creatures that wander the roads.

Unlike deer that are fast and agile, there is absolutely nothing about cows that says speed. They can move when they want to … but mostly, they lumber through life, seemingly unaware. As creatures of habit, one of their beloved moves is to lay on the asphalt after the sun goes down, soaking up the heat of the day. They are not concerned about what's coming around the bend.

Hitting any of the above-mentioned animals could result in severe damage and personal injury to man, beast, and the Postage Stamp. We decided getting there in one piece was far more critical. I also began to notice all the crosses and monuments on the side of the road marking the passing of those who had driven this brutal stretch of highway.

About thirty minutes later, we were in Los Barriles and so grateful. Perhaps not seeing the road and the reasons for the detours that had us driving ever so slowly—and at times in stretches of sand—was better. We would learn later that the road to La Paz is perilously tricky due to its hairpin corners and sheer drop-offs. It took us two hours that night and was something akin to off-road driving. With every bump, I tensed up, and I could not help wondering what we would find strewn about the Postage Stamp when we finally reached Number Six.

Michael decided slow and late was better than dead and on time. When we arrived in Los Barriles, we breathed a collective sigh. We had done it. We were tired, emotionally spent, hungry, and suffering from car face. Now all we needed to do was find the RV park. How hard could that be? According to GPS, we were thirty minutes away.

What? Thirty more minutes? To be sure, GPS does not always work in Mexico so we decided to ask.

We pulled into the local Pemex gas station to ask for directions. Michael climbed out of the truck and glanced over to his right. Eureka! The RV Park was directly across the street. He started laughing and pointing. Only five-and-a-half days ago, we had left Vancouver Island. Here we were at last. We had done it and already had stories to tell and memories to treasure.

For us, the RV park was the most beautiful sight at that moment, not because of its aesthetics but because we were finally there. Once through the big iron gates, we drove directly to Number Six.

Jumping out of the truck with the energy of two five-year-old kids, we took a deep, cleansing breath. Mia Mukluks seemed to know we had finally arrived and was singing and dancing in her crate. Michael unlatched her door, and she propelled herself to the ground in sheer joy. At the same time, Grumpy Tequila remained disinterested, lounging sleepily in his crate, only slightly opening one eye as if to say, "What's all the commotion about?"

Tossing my flip-flops aside, the coolness of the sand beneath my feet surprised me. Michael was over the sea wall and walking down to the shoreline in a flash. I wanted to imprint this moment on my mind forever. The briny mist, so salty and sweet, gently kissed my lips. The stars filled the night sky and seemed to dip into the sea.

Michael shouted from the shore. "Hey, come down here and check this out!"

The moonlight's glow was in harmony at the shoreline, rolling in and out with the tide. There were lights in the distance, and they, too, seemed to dance on the water. It was as though everything had been orchestrated to welcome us to our adventure.

Mia Mukluks was now running in circles showing us her best tricks. Meanwhile, we stood peering into the night in disbelief. *We had made it.* There would be plenty of time to celebrate, but we were content to stand and take it all in tonight.

The road trip to Los Barriles is like nothing most people will ever experience. If I had to describe it in two sentences, I would say: It's harsh, mystical, ethereal, and primarily untamed. It must be shared with another courageous soul to understand.

And, of course, a road trip through any country will open your eyes and heart. Helping appreciate what is, lending way to perspective, and understanding our impact and smallness in the world. We were privileged to have driven through Australia, Canada, and the United States through the years. But none of that could compare to what we had just lived and seen.

Site Number Six

*W*e woke to the sound of palm leaves on the window from the breeze off the ocean. It was dawn, and a new day beckoned; it was surreal after so much planning and driving. We were settling in at Number Six in Los Barriles—there would be no rushing today.

The day called for relaxation and nothing more. Michael made coffee as I made my high-test tea and toast, slathered with extra butter and topped with orange ginger marmalade. Michael and I deemed Grumpy Tequila the best traveler of all. He lay stretched out fully on the loveseat, watching sleepily as we puttered about in the kitchen.

The sky came alive, from grey to burnt orange and pink; it was breathtaking. It was my very favorite time of day playing out before my eyes. As the morning light began to seep into the Postage Stamp, the walls took on the color of the sky, becoming a kaleidoscope of colors dancing.

Thoroughly steeped, I poured the strong tea into my favorite mug and an earthy aroma filled the air; this was one of those perfect moments in life; one you reflect on in the dark times and realize this moment made it all worthwhile.

With tea, toast, and my camera, the Two Traveling Fools and Mia Mukluks headed out the door. Tequila didn't move. He had no interest in watching the sunrise. And, in usual cat fashion, he looked at us as if to say, "Seriously?!"

The fresh ocean air filled my lungs as I stepped out of the Stamp. We spread out the blanket on the rock wall for comfort and swung our legs over our front row seat while I sipped my tea.

Here, we sat less than 15 meters (50 feet) offshore. Even Mia Mukluks seemed mesmerized as she sat with us on the wall, gazing out to sea as the sun came up. Suddenly, it hit me, and every part of my being was tingling; tears of joy began to leak from my eyes. Mia Mukluks came over and positioned herself between us, and we all sat in silence … watching the world awaken.

One after one, the anglers returned with their morning catch. Seagulls soared overhead, waiting for the perfect chance to swoop down and grab breakfast. Roosters woke and began to crow, signifying a new day had begun. Not to be left behind; some local dogs joined the chorus. It was nature's morning song, beckoning all to rise for a new day.

Just as the sun popped up above the horizon, birds began to sing. I glimpsed a hummingbird hovering only feet away from us. Words were not needed.

Today was about celebrating and being in gratitude and grace. We had made it from our front door in Canada to Number Six in five-and-a-half days. On the way back, it would be different; we had so many places to explore.

The day ahead was about staking out Number Six, our little piece of paradise on the beach. Although there would be a lot to do, we had all the time we needed. We shifted from rushed and hurried to calm and purposeful.

The temperature for the day ahead was to be a sweltering 32°C (90°F) with 54 percent humidity and a light wind of 10 kilometers (6 miles). At 11:00 a.m., I caught a glimpse of my first mirage dancing off the sandy shore; it was time to play in the water.

As we headed to the seawall, Mia Mukluks took no time flat to make the distance. She ran ahead and launched herself, Supergirl-style onto the sand and headed straight into the sea. All she needed was a cape to make the scene perfect. We both stood laughing. Who'd have thought a dog who, only a year before, was terrified of waves gently lapping the river's shoreline would run into the sea now at full speed? Michael followed nearly as fast, diving into the crystal-clear waters. He swam out for what seemed like forever. When he surfaced, he yelled back to me on shore, "OMG—it's like bathwater!"

I strolled down to join them, dipping my toes in slowly. It's not that Michael was not to be trusted with gauging temperature, but I am generally cold and like to ease myself in. As soon as I stepped into the water, the warmth of the sea enveloped me; Michael was right. It was just like bathwater. And the pristine cerulean blue was stunning.

We returned to shore refreshed and charmed. This was so much more than I had ever imagined. Michael squeezed my hand as though he knew what I was thinking, I turned to look at him; his neck and ear still bore the scar of the siphonophore. I was reminded of how far we had come. I knew I would be forever drawn to the Sea of Cortez. Setting up our chairs and beach blanket, we sat and quickly fell sound asleep. We woke to the rays of the sun's intense heat. It was too hot to do much of anything outside, so we went inside to continue setting things up.

Siesta is generally during the hottest time of the day, between 2:00 and 5:00 p.m. Our earlier beach nap had refreshed us and we worked inside. We returned to the task of setting up our outdoor living area after the heat of the day had passed. Meanwhile, the park manager arrived to erect two bamboo walls on our site, creating a cozy, intimate space and shelter from the wind.

As the sun gave way to the moon, we sat enjoying the sounds of the sea. Within minutes, we were again amid the backdrop of the starry night sky.

The following day, we woke again to the brilliant pinks of the sky filling the Postage Stamp. We discovered during our research on Baja that nary a day is different weather-wise and on average there are 350 days of sunshine here each year. We also read about hurricane season and when one hits this area, it's crazy, dangerous, and in some cases, catastrophic. Tropical storms hit, too, and can deluge the area with buckets of rain in a heartbeat. With nowhere for the water to flow, streets become flooded so people grab their paddleboards and kayaks to get around. What a sight!

Still, no two days are alike. Sunrise is more than the sun rising; it's a way of living, an attitude, a promise of a new day. And we were not going to miss anything.

Over the next three days, we continued to set up Number Six. Every area was carefully considered and discussed as though we were building a future home. The placement of mats, outdoor furniture, the BBQ, evening lighting, and our paddleboards was of utmost importance to the site's functionality.

We must have looked very serious and professional.

"Are you two house stagers?" a woman passing by asked.

We laughed and said no. However, we were determined and dedicated to ensuring the best use of our homestead on the beach.

After a quick introduction, we learned that Margaret had cycled from Vancouver, Canada, to Los Barriles. And we had thought we were daring? Not even close. What we were was naïve. While glamping in luxury on our way down the Baja Peninsula, Margaret was roughing it in every sense of the word! She was determined and nothing stopped her; she was compelled and knew it was now or never.

Not only did Margaret ride the same roads we did, but she traversed them on her eighteen-speed bicycle. She rode for hours in the hot sun, over mountain passes, dodging potholes, cars, and massive tractor-trailer trucks on skinny roads, oh, and let's not forget the snakes and other road critters. At the end of each day, she found a spot off-road, rolled out her tent and slept on the ground. Nothing like a bit of humility to straighten you out!

She said it had always been a dream to bike to Baja. I was in complete awe of her strength, courage, and determination. Having only recently retired at sixty years old, Margret felt if she didn't do it now, she might never do it. She told us she was passing through Los Barriles on her way west to Todos Santos on the Pacific Side.

Did I mention she was sixty?

My friend Kim Duke says that "life is the complicated simple." I tell you, Margaret embodied everything about the complicated simple. We thought our drive down was challenging? She carried everything she needed on her back and above her wheels: tent, sleeping bag, mat, clothes, water, and snacks.

I asked her what the most challenging part of the ride was, expecting her to say the lack of shoulders, the potholes, the blind corners, or the crazy traffic, but she never mentioned any of that. No. What Margret said caught me off guard.

"The dogs that would try to attack me were the most frightening and difficult part of the ride."

The dogs?

To Eat or Not to Eat

There is a misperception about traveling and living in another place. One of life's great ironies is that we are the same wherever we go, no matter how much we desire to be different. The same habits and beliefs follow us as we do the same tasks. Someone wise once put it this way, "Wherever I go, there I am."

Groceries need buying, beds need making—even if that only means throwing the duvet haphazardly over the bed and plumping pillows for later slumber—and meals need cooking. That's life. After a few days of setting up Number Six, it was time to venture out to get provisions.

As we left the park on the ATV heading into town to find the big grocery store and the hardware store, Michael let out a "yahoo!" Where else can you drive an off-road vehicle through the streets? In Los Barriles, it is a common practice.

We were given precise and concise directions to get to the local grocery store. "Take the back road by the hotel into town, beware of the blind corners as some drivers forget it's two lanes, once on the pavement, turn left and go up the hill to Chapitos market on the right." *Got it.*

There are only a few paved roads in Los Barriles so, in this case, the directions were easy to follow. The back road was interesting, which is a code word for scary. Not only was the road narrow with hairpin turns but a large chain-link fence, that no doubt at one time been erect, was partially laying on the road at a blind corner making the road even more challenging. I made a mental note never to drive or walk it at night. On the right, was the Chapitos; perhaps I had misunderstood.

This store reminded me of the old Red & White grocery store chain from my youth.

Michael was on a mission to find a local hardware store. We were surprised to learn from another couple that we could find a Home Depot, two Walmart stores, and a Costco in Cabo San Lucas, only an hour-and-a-half away. However, our goal was to support local businesses and only shop at big box stores if necessary.

I grabbed a carry basket with my list in hand, thinking I would pick up a few things today. It was both odd and ordinary. I was in Mexico shopping for groceries just as I would in Canada. But I wasn't in Canada, which did not escape me. It was all so surreal.

The store, albeit smaller than the supermarkets back home, seemed well stocked. As I entered, on my left were toys and a *papeleria* section for stationery, complete with balloons and other party favors, followed by a clothing section, kitchen supplies, and lots more. I was surprised to see a row of appliances, and the back wall had shelves lined with a variety of spirits and beer. It was an all-purpose store stocked with a little bit of everything. The food isles were also full, even though most contained brands I had never seen or heard of before.

There was an aisle stocked with brands and products I did know: mayonnaise, yellow mustard, ketchup, box cakes, and a few different kinds of cereals, pasta, and rice.

I was mesmerized by the many brands offered but decided to start with produce and made my way back. As I was about to exit the aisle, I heard a woman's voice. "You're in the *gringo* aisle."

I turned to see who was speaking to me. A woman, who I presumed to be in her late sixties, was standing behind me—her skin golden-brown from the sun—dressed in shorts and a fancy t-shirt. Her hair was perfectly coifed, her jewelry appeared heavy on her petite frame, and her feet were beautifully showcased in sandals fit for a cruise ship. It was clear to me she spent a great deal of time dressing.

On the other hand, I had messy hair tied up in a ponytail that was windblown from riding on the back of the ATV, with strands escaping from every which way. My well-worn t-shirt, shorts, and flip-flops were disheveled and more "beachwear" at best. Apparently, I was not adequately dressed for the store.

"Pardon me?" I asked.

"The gringo aisle," she repeated.

I laughed nervously, not sure how to respond. With that, she left me standing in the aisle. Perhaps my nervous giggle convinced her I was out of my depth, and I was. As I stepped out of the aisle, another woman, dressed more like myself, was rounding the corner. I'm not sure why that mattered, but it did at the moment.

The produce section was two aisles away. The display was not fancy or set in the way I was used to seeing, but it was as inviting as unassuming. What I found was the freshest and most beautiful produce. The colors beckoned me, especially carrots, celery, chilies, lettuce, peppers, and herbs. I was inspired to try everything—well, maybe not everything. We enjoy spicy food, but our exposure is primarily limited to dishes made in Canada, meaning our palates are not "spiceitized," as I like to say.

I had never seen so many different chilies in all colors, shapes, and sizes. Later, I learned that more than 150 varieties of chilies are grown in Mexico, with flavors ranging from earthy, sweet, and smoky to the hottest of hot. Chilies are used in almost every dish but, to my surprise, not always for heat. Based on our limited exposure and Canadian palate, I decided to stick with the chilies we knew. In Mexico, *jalapeño* and *serrano* peppers are far down on the heat and spice index.

The avocados were beautifully fleshy, large, and perfectly ripe. I may have made a joyful noise when I spotted the overflowing bins of cilantro. I felt like a kid in a candy store of green goodness. Before I knew it, my carry basket was full of fresh veggies. So much so that I had to go back and get a shopping cart on wheels.

Setting my carry basket into the cart, I continued my maiden tour of the store, a cornucopia of foods I had never experienced. Each aisle offered something new, and although not familiar, still looked interesting. Almost everything was labeled in Spanish, and why wouldn't it be?

I came from the land of plenty with big box stores and multiple selections; I was used to being able to access almost anything. Here, choices were more limited, but so be it. I wasn't here to be the same as I was in Canada and knew this was part of my Mexico experience. As Michael likes to say, we were being "Mexicanated," and there is no better way to become Mexicanated than going all in.

The cheese display, known as *queso*, was enormous for such a small store. There were so many cheeses, all from different regions, but oddly, there was no cheddar. Equally impressive was the selection of refried beans, which are finished with a specific cheese. Cheese is a crucial ingredient in many dishes, especially my favorite, *quesadillas*.

Grilled cheese is simply a cheese *quesadilla* in Mexico when it comes down to it. As I studied the cheese, I decided to buy five different kinds. We would need to do a formal cheese test from crumbly to sliced. Again, something new to experience and enjoy. Our adventure was going to be filled with cheesy delight.

Next was *mantequilla*, the butter, one of my most beloved food groups. Yes, food groups. I am very passionate about butter, so this is a must-have. I think life without butter would lack depth and substance.

There is nothing better than homemade bread, sliced fresh from the oven and slathered with butter and raspberry jam. Yum!

Aside from butter being rather costly, it is primarily sold *sin sal,* meaning without salt. No problem. I could add Himalayan salt, which is infinitely better for you. I checked off everything on my list and added much more to the cart.

Now, I had to figure out how to get all the bags home while I rode on the back of the ATV. I realized I hadn't thought that part through. Michael returned to pick me up and smiled at my bounty and all the juggling I had to do to get ready for the ride. He was thrilled to have found a local hardware store. It was one I knew he would visit many times during our time at Number Six.

Back at camp, we unpacked eagerly. We were both hungry and excited to start our culinary adventure. I prepared a *charcuterie* board of Mexican deliciousness. I began with sliced avocado, all five kinds of cheese, and extra cilantro. The star of the display was a bowl of fresh *pico de gallo*, another of my favorite things in Mexico. On a serving board, I placed two small white ceramic bowls full of reheated refried beans, accompanied by four divinely-fresh flour tortillas we had picked up at a tortilla factory along the way.

oll

Tales of the Road

*W*e continued our ritual of rising at dawn to watch the sun come up. Arriving at the beginning of November is incredibly early in the season for snowbirds, so we mostly had the park to ourselves. Only a handful of us would be there for the entire season, which typically spans five to six months.

We met some of the most memorable people at the park. It was like living in a global village of wanderlust for life. Many, to our surprise, came to Baja from Europe by sea, which meant shipping their motorhomes in containers on cargo ships. This gave me pause; imagine driving your motorhome and belongings into a shipping container—your only means of transportation—and hoping it would arrive on the other side of the world. People came from Germany, Spain, the United Kingdom, and beyond. Some traveled seven to a camper, ranging from three months to eighty-eight years old. All had the same dream to live beachside that year.

Perspective is the insight into our perceived challenge. Knowing and doing are different, and knowing how far these people had come grounded us both. We also met others from Canada and the United States who had driven Mex 1. Some families had planned and saved for two years to realize this dream. Parents and grandparents had committed to homeschooling their children and grandchildren.

The motorhomes, trailers, and campers were as varied as the people. European-manufactured motorhomes are the most interesting. They resemble armored cars and war tanks, and they are amazingly efficient and roadworthy. And some can sleep up to eight. When fully opened, they are the Ikea of travel design.

One couple we met, Cathy and Tony, were from Manchester, England. This was their second season at the park and they occupied Site Number Eleven, along with their beloved pooch, Benjamin. Number Eleven was next to the *palapa* on stilts that became a sanctuary to watch the sunrise, sip tea, and chat. Mia Mukluks fell instantly in love with Benjamin. Both dogs ran in circles, jumping over each other, stopping instantly, and sending sand flying everywhere. The laughter from the four of us only fueled their crazy antics.

Cathy and Tony's story of shipping their motorhome from England to Mexico was eye-opening. They arrived, and yet their motorhome did not. Coming in May, as per the instructions for a smooth transition, they were shocked when they were informed via email it would be another month before their motorhome arrived. They had two small suitcases of clothes and Benjamin and believed it would work out as planned. There is no 1-800 number to call and get concise answers when shipping your motorhome. Smooth shipping depends on calm seas and no hurricanes, tropical storms, or other unforeseen issues.

They had done all they could, so they decided to make the best of it and vacationed in La Paz while waiting. Thirty days later, they finally got the call, and all was good. These two were brave souls coming to a faraway land and trusting it would all work out. What else could go wrong? Well, aside from what they had just overcome, Baja is both hot and humid in June, and it is the beginning of the tropical storm season. That June, the hundred-year rains had hit Baja. It was a tropical storm that was relentless.

I knew a little something about tropical storms. While in Costa Rica in 2000, I witnessed a tropical storm event; it's not to be underestimated. One minute it was sunny, and the streets were filled with shoppers carrying their packages and enjoying the day. The outdoor cafés and patios were filled. I watched a young mother and her daughter sitting in the shade of the patio umbrella, enjoying an ice-cream sundae, and laughing.

Suddenly, the air was cool, and dark clouds moved in. People left the streets, heading inside or scrambling to ensure cover. At that moment, two entrepreneurial young men appeared streetside selling umbrellas as though they were clairvoyant. I thought it odd but noticed the mother and daughter were also gone.

I naïvely laughed at all the commotions of what was likely only to be a fall rain shower. I bought an umbrella to support the young men who seemed to be potentially capitalizing on the weather. The cost was $3.00, a small price to pay.

As though on cue, the wind whipped up, making it difficult to see and, in some cases, breathe. Flying objects that would otherwise be nothing more than a nuisance became deadly weapons, followed by the rains. Large, angry drops of rain became progressively larger and fell faster and faster until a deluge of water was creating instant rivers. And this, I discovered, is why almost all tropical countries have sidewalks that are at least a foot tall.

The sky became darker and darker, and all the daylight seemed to disappear, as though nightfall was upon us. The sounds were equally frightening. With each gust of wind, trees snapped like twigs, the palms bent to the ground and back, and those that didn't break seemed like they were in a raging fight to live. In the middle of such a storm, it is loud and terrifying.

Once the rains began, my newly purchased umbrella lasted all of five minutes as the wind inverted it. Now, it was an upside-down bowl catching rain and being ripped from side to side. I must have been a pitiful sight: a middle-aged woman hanging on for dear life to her umbrella. The next gust of wind broke the shaft, carrying the inverted canopy away. There I stood, dripping wet, holding the handgrip and stainless-steel shaft. It's funny now, but it wasn't then.

I heard a voice in the wind and saw a hand motioning me to come in. As I stood shivering, the glow of embarrassment warmed my cheeks. My thin white t-shirt and pants were now see-through. Thankfully, my embarrassment warmed me up. So much for a fall rain shower.

I could only imagine what Cathy and Tony had experienced. I have no desire to experience a hurricane; being in a motorhome on a beach with the sea raging less than 15 meters (50 feet) away would have been terrifying.

Storms, be they tropical or hurricanes, can only be experienced to fully understand the wreaked devastation and havoc. Unless you have been in the eye of a tropical storm, it's hard to imagine the impact of constant and relentless rain. As a result, the ground begins to lose its ability to drain. First puddles form. Not cute puddles that are fun to play in but pools that are deep and wide and soon become rivers, so much so that the streets fill up.

Over the months, Cathy and Tony became fast friends, and many laughs were shared and we would meet other like-minded people who came to Baja exploring and fell in love.

We continued to meet many other folks who were retired and had been preparing for their epic journeys. There were no limits to the highway horror stories shared around fires at night. The stories were as varied as the people who told them. Some suffered catastrophic damage to their RV when it dropped a foot off the road as they pulled off onto what they thought was the shoulder. Some stories are too crazy to fathom. If we hadn't heard them from those who had personally experienced them, we would have thought them to be folklore.

Such was the case with Kristy and Brock. Almost all recreational vehicles include slides—hard-sided pop-out areas—to enhance your enjoyment and space. Slides are retracted during road travel as they are meant only to be out when your RV is set up. Kristy and Brock's story about them is enough to make anyone cringe.

They had woken early to watch the sunrise where they were camping at Playa Santispac. They were planning to leave that morning, and began readying their motorhome for travel. Kristy walked around, checking the lockers and such, and noticed a large pool of purple fluid collecting beneath the slide on the passenger side. It was hydraulic fluid, and it looked like all of it was on the ground.

She and Brock quickly surmised that it was impossible to put the slide in electrically or manually. They found out the closest hydraulic mechanic was three hours away. They had no choice but to unhook the tow car for Kristy to follow behind Brock as he drove with the slide hanging out. The open slide took up an additional meter or so (about 3 feet) of the lane, which was already narrow. Brock, a retired pilot, drove precisely, narrowly missing signs and many big rigs. When they arrived at the shop three hours later, they were informed they needed a specialty hydraulics mechanic who was, naturally, located much farther away.

They went back on the road, getting many bewildered looks from locals who undoubtedly thought they had forgotten to put the slide in. After countless hours of driving, they found who they needed, and they were able to stay onsite for the night while everything was fixed. Driving with a slide open is very dangerous, but their story is an excellent reminder of the adaptability, ingenuity, and dogged determination required to live life fully.

After hearing the harrowing and, at times, hilarious stories of traffic jams created by goats and cows, near misses, and equipment failure, we realized we had pretty much come through the trip unscathed. With one exception, our near-death experience. Maybe epic adventures are meant to be experienced and not plotted out in advance to include every possible hazard. Perhaps being a little naïve at times is its own blessing. What we knew for sure is everyone's journey is different and some moments along the way are more memorable than others.

Wherefore Art Thou Wind?

*M*ichael was beginning to get antsy; he longed to get back on the water. First, he needed to get equipment and take more lessons. His goal was to kite every day the wind was blowing. Timing is everything; the winds had not yet picked up and likely wouldn't until late November.

This gave Michael the much-needed time to get his kiting equipment. There is no better place to purchase what he needed than in a kiting community. The equipment is top-notch, and often last year's models are deeply discounted.

He traveled to La Ventana to see his friend, a former firefighter colleague from Canada and his first kite instructor, for a visit and to purchase his equipment. When he arrived back at Number Six, he was ecstatic, smiling from ear to ear as he filled me in on the day's events. He proudly showed me all his new equipment. He had purchased a kiteboard, a twin tip, a kite retrieval leash, a seat harness, a bar and lines, and two kites: an 8 meter (26 foot) and a 12 meter (39 foot). The velocity of the wind determines the size of the kite to use.

This was it; he was all set now. He just needed wind. He checked the various wind predictors for the next week and a half to see if this would be the day. But no wind came. As days went by, his longing grew.

And then it happened. The wind predictors began to register winds and he booked his first of eight refresher lessons.

Kiteboarding is like learning to ride a bike, only without training wheels. You fly over the ocean with 1–3-meter (4–10-foot) waves and wind gusts of up to 45 kilometers (28 miles) per hour. Well, come to think of it, kiteboarding is nothing like riding a bike—nothing at all. It takes hours and hours to master and it isn't for the faint of heart.

His first day was spent getting reacquainted with the various kite techniques, including kite control, safety protocols, and becoming familiar with his new equipment. His early lessons had him launch the board from a seated to a standing position, leveraging the kite for power. He practiced for hours and hours until it became second nature.

Once Michael completed his lessons, he and a buddy would help each other launch and discuss "how to." After that, it's all about time spent on the water, practicing and refining. There is no easy softer way; the only way to master kiting is to pay your dues. Michael had many days of frustration and disappointment early on. But he never gave up, and each day was a new day to try again.

Seasoned kiters will tell you that everyone will have their share of wins and kitemares. Only other kiters understand a language spoken between them, and Michael was embracing it all. I have heard wives say they were kite widows; it meant their spouse was always kiting. I mostly never minded—unless I wanted to go exploring, but then we just worked it out.

Although we enjoy each other's company, being together twenty-four seven wears on even the most fun-loving couples. I, too, longed for the wind. As my mom used to say, "People get on each other's nerves," and our tiny home was very tight.

Great Expectations

*T*he day came when the wind arrived, and she stayed. The wind blew daily and it created space for me to unpack my office, untangle my thoughts, and embrace all that lay before me.

Pretty soon, we had new routines. We played ball with Mia Mukluks on the beach and then paddle boarded, snorkeled, swam, or walked before the waves picked up and returned, mainly before 10:00 in the morning, to enjoy a late breakfast. After that, Michael would ready his kiting equipment and head out the door by noon, often not returning until after 4:00 p.m.

Kiting is beautiful and terrifying to watch as the wind pulls each kiter out to sea. With brightly colored kites, it is as though they are performing a perfectly choreographed scene in the sky. Most kiters are young and fit, some are older, and some courageous souls are in their wisdom years when they learn to master the sport. Ask a kiter how it feels to launch and power up the kite, jump, ride the waves, depower the kite, return to where they started, and their answers range from sheer joy to terror. Michael was truly in his element.

In those hours, I had the Stamp all to myself. I could dance, read, write, listen to my music, watch my favorite Netflix shows, or relax. Mia Mukluks and Tequila remained with me, often sprawled out on the sofa with little movement, only opening their eyes if they heard a noise other than me.

I am a creature of habit, and although I do not drink coffee—I am a lover of loose-leaf tea—I consume eight to ten cups of tea a day. I like my tea over-steeped in a French press. The brew is a high-test, pungent, bitter tea that makes your mouth pucker as though the tannins are screaming at you. As a writer, tea is my necessary companion, but it has been my addiction since I was eight years old.

Until the winds came consistently, I had been mostly off the grid and enjoying every moment. But then, the itch to write came upon me, and so began my love affair with writing in Baja. It was time to set up my mobile office, complete with a video recording station. Inspiration for writing and working remotely, I was told, would be easily accessed through the camp's Wi-Fi. Well, it was accessible but not fully functional.

And there was a challenge; although you can access the internet with Wi-Fi, that is only the first step. One of the first lessons on living in Mexico and working remotely: there is a caveat. Coming from Canada, I mistakenly assumed (*I know, wrong*) that using Wi-Fi in Mexico would be somewhat similar. It is not.

First and foremost, Wi-Fi is available and affordable but often only through cellular towers. This causes a multitude of challenges when using video-conferencing apps like Zoom or Skype. Of course, a cell phone can be used as a hotspot. But if your setting is on roaming from Canada or the United States, the price is a small mortgage payment.

We learned quickly about the advantages of unlocking a phone and opening a Mexican account with a local phone number, another step in becoming Mexicanated. The local plans are amazingly affordable and functional, but they aren't great for hot-spotting, a strange term that sounds illegal, but it isn't in any way.

The best way to set up Wi-Fi is to get a wireless modem. The modems work off cell towers, which can be problematic at times. Ensuring stable signals and connections for streaming services can be a test of patience. Though the monthly plans are economical and allow multiple devices, it can be a hit-and-miss situation, especially during high winds. But before too long, I was back in business, operating from Baja. Yay!

At first, working remotely in Mexico seemed unattainable but we figured it out. Although working from home wasn't new to me, in Mexico, I had to adapt my expectations and get creative. Planning and hosting live events can be done anywhere if the Wi-Fi is fully functional. After Michael shared his idea about wintering in Mexico, I concocted a big, audacious dream to host live voluntourism events internationally while based in Mexico.

Once we worked out all the technical hiccups, I was all set. We established a routine, days ran into weeks, and each day was much like the last. Before we knew it, it was mid-November. When Michael went kiting, I hunkered down with pen in hand and strategized about all the things we could do at a live event here in Mexico.

Those Eyes!

The community market opened the third week of November, and I was forever changed. Michael and I went to look for Christmas gifts to take to family and friends in Canada. We would be flying back to Canada for a few weeks in December for the holidays. Then, I saw her out of the corner of my eye.

Inside the large wire pen, among the other pups, she sat. Her big chocolate eyes followed me everywhere. I was drawn to her. There she was, staring at me, and pulling me closer. She was mostly tan with black tips on her ears and near her mouth. She was indeed a Baja Pup. Judging by her size and demeanor, I thought she was two months old. The entire time I watched her, she remained seated, just waiting for someone to love her. I couldn't help myself; I went to find out about this sweet pup.

As I walked toward her, I made the ridiculous kissy-face sounds grown adults often do when they see a baby. I mean, how could I not? She was adorable! And those eyes! Soon she was on her hind legs begging to be picked up. Her name, Chica. Of course, it was. Chica most often means sweet little girl.

I was instantly smitten. After showering me with kisses, she stared at me—her big brown eyes seeking love and acceptance. My heart was melting. Michael knows me so well. Before I could say a word, he emphatically stated. "We cannot adopt another dog right now; it's not fair to Tequila or Mia Mukluks." Of course, I knew he was right, but I hated that he was.

At that moment, I wanted to scoop up Chica and bring her back to Number Six. Chica had been abandoned and left to die in the *arroyo*. If not for Cortez Rescue finding and rescuing her, she would have died. At that moment, I knew we had to do something bigger, but I had no idea what.

That night we talked about the plight of the many dogs and cats who are abandoned here. We decided that although we couldn't adopt, we could foster some dogs. So, we did. We began with a couple of strays, and then Riley came, along with others. And every time they left us, I sobbed, not because I wanted to adopt them but because their hearts had imprinted on our hearts.

There is a saying in rescue: if you can't adopt, foster, and if you can't foster, donate. At the very least, we could foster. We also signed up to be flight angels. Essentially, you take a dog to its forever home when flying home from Mexico.

Surprisingly, Tequila took it all in stride, although if any of the pups were too rambunctious, he would look at us as if to say, "Are you kidding?" Mia Mukluks was mainly thrilled to have sleepovers with friends. But even she had her limits with the youngest ones, once they were healthy enough to play and pounce on her.

We fostered from then on. I have lost track of how many we have fostered and helped find forever homes, but it never gets old, and the need is real. Mexicali remains the most fragile of all the pups we have fostered. She was better friends with Tequila because she was a spitfire full of life, and once healthy, Mexicali enjoyed jumping continuously on Mia Mukluks, however, the enjoyment was not mutual.

Mexicali unexpectedly came to us while volunteering at SNAP, a spay, neuter, awareness prevention initiative. She weighed only ounces, less than a pound, and her opaque light blue eyes suggested she was blind. She had been left in a brown paper sack outside the clinic in the sun. Had she not been found she would surely have died that day. The vet was kind but also truthful about her chances of survival. Dr. Cristobal was not sure Mexicali would make it, but he was sure she was blind.

We decided to foster her. What she needed and deserved was to be loved. She was dumped due to no fault of her own. Honestly, I wasn't sure she would make it through that first night, but she did, and every day she grew more robust and spunkier. Before we knew it, she had gained weight and was thriving. She wasn't blind, but instead, she suffered the impact of malnutrition so severely that the blood supply had gone to her vital organs. Once her tiny body was no longer in a state of survival, she regained her ability to see. Mexicali now lives in her forever home in Vancouver, Canada, with her family.

When we hosted the foster pups, the tiny home shrunk, or so it seemed, yet it became filled with more joy than ever. One little girl, Mimi, came and stole our hearts. She was adopted and only needed a home for a couple of weeks until she flew on to her forever home. Mimi, a chihuahua cross about three years old, had far too many puppies for her young age and was grossly underweight.

She settled right in and played with Mia Mukluks for hours. They used the bed as a trampoline, and it was all kinds of hilarious. The minute Michael stirred in the morning, Mimi seemed to know a new day had begun. Unlike most dogs, when first waking, Mimi didn't go outside until she had expressed her joy and gratitude.

As soon as Michael opened the crate, Mimi would run full tilt and launch herself onto the bed to deliver kisses and share her unbridled gratitude for us. Then, she and Mia Mukluks would commence the circle game on the bed with me tucked safely under the feather duvet. The more I laughed, the faster they went.

When it was time for Mimi to go to her forever home, although I was so happy for her, I broke down and cried, then cried some more. Mimi had shown us all, love heals. She was a dog who just wanted to belong. After Mimi left to go to her forever home, Grumpy Tequila and Mia Mukluks looked for her for days, staring out the window, sulking and looking at us suspiciously as if to ask, "Where is she?" Mimi, in such short time, had become family.

We learned deeply about ourselves and others from fostering. I knew that although we had come to winter in Baja, it became so much more. There is always a need to be fulfilled in any community, and it gave us great purpose. So, we began to volunteer more, in between beaching, snorkeling, living, paddling, kiting, writing, and working.

The Serendipitous Accident

*G*etting to know others in Mexico is reminiscent of youth where location and interests seem to bridge any gaps. The conversations flow easily for the most part, and, as the saying goes: like attracts like. Although we come from various parts of the world, we all have Los Barriles in common. Mexico and its culture attract people from all walks of life. Perhaps it's that draw that truly bridges all gaps. After all, we are all visitors to this country and blessed to be so.

Whenever I meet someone, I wonder what brought them to Baja. Remarkably, the answer is almost always they are here by accident. I think we all come here exploring and many fall in love. Perhaps it's more serendipitous than accidental—more divine than earthly. Most of the people we meet are heart-centered, driven to serve, and active community members.

Sure, some come on vacation, happy to just sit seaside and enjoy the margaritas and delicious Mexican cuisine. Everyone contributes, whether they be adventure seekers, kiters, or vacationers, to the economy and atmosphere, creating a beautiful community of people simply living out their dreams *while they can*.

We sensed a shift in December, which turned into a busy month. Each day would bring more people to the RV park until they couldn't squeeze any more in. Soon, the park was packed. With so much in common, friendships flourished, and in the evening, the place would be filled with laughter and stories of the day's adventures.

Those who arrive by early December generally stay until the season ends in late April, so we become quasi-family for each other. In these active months, the sleepy little fishing village becomes fully awake and buzzing. The streets are filled with locals, ex-pats, and visitors navigating the narrow roads on ATVs, alongside cars and trucks. The town goes from a population of 2,000 to 10,000 in a matter of weeks. All the seasonal stores reopen, and people fill the streets night and day.

Los Barriles transformed into much more than I had imagined; there were no shortage of things to see and do daily. Many organized daily activities for those not kiting or relaxing on the beach were centered around fun and fundraising—which I love.

Every night seemed to be a feature night. Our favorites were Sunday night dinners at Tio Pablo's, Monday night salsa lessons, Wednesday nights at La Fugato for Open Mic, and Thursday nights often featured one of the most accomplished guitarists in Mexico at Beans and Rice. Occasionally, we'd spend Friday nights at the La Playa for live music. Even more monthly events were held in our community square. The *cancha, aka* the basketball court, has movie night once a month featuring some of the latest releases. There is something to do every day and every night for those who love to be out and about.

Keep in mind, the average age of those who visit Los Barriles is over fifty, so "midnight" comes early at 9:00 p.m. Even the cows seem to understand and respect Baja Midnight. As the streets seemingly roll up, the cows reclaim them, and saunter in rhythm. All in all, most events and dinners start early and end early, all adding to the charm of Los Barriles.

Friendships are easily forged, too. It's how we met many dear friends, who we now call our Baja sisters and brothers. First, it was Celeste and Steve, and then Cheryl and Bill, who indeed are our Baja family. Whether here or apart, we are connected and cheering each other on. With so much in common, friendships are not about location or proximity to each other but rather about a deep knowing we are all here by choice and living our best lives, *while we can.*

During our short time here this first season, we'd already learned so much. In Mexico, the culture is less about acquisition and more about appreciation; less is truly more. Appreciation of manners and how you are is far more critical than what you wish to acquire. Mexico has a deep appreciation of relationships and the human condition. Value is placed on connection and respect. Items, although appreciated, hold less weight and value than that of the relationship.

At least from what we had experienced so far, Mexican life was relatively simple unless we chose to complicate it. The lifestyle can best be described as hard-working, polite, and fun-loving. Family and friends are an integral part of life, and enjoying the outdoors surpasses any material possessions.

Soon enough, it was time for our interim trip home. Leaving Grumpy Tequila and our tiny home felt oddly strange as we packed for our Christmas visit. We were excited to see our family and friends in Canada for the holidays, yet it seemed as though we had only just arrived here in our little paradise. Now, we were leaving behind the new friends and lifestyle we had so quickly fallen into—and in love with.

Bone Cold

$\mathcal{W}$ith a mug of tea in hand, we walked hand in hand to the shoreline. Standing in the cool sand as the waves gently lapped the shore, our feet sank deeper and deeper into the sand with each wave. Perhaps it was just the romance of the Sea of Cortez but at that moment, I had a vision of Michael and me serving more intentionally.

I also knew significant changes were coming, yet I had no idea what they were. Maybe Michael felt it too, but he said nothing.

The sunrise that morning was a beautiful rainbow of pink and orange; it was breathtaking. Morning light brings new promise, and the most spectacular of sunrises are where sun and clouds share the morning sky. As we stood planted with the sand squishing between our toes, the sun popped up over the horizon, and a brand-new day had begun. It was time for us to return to the trailer and get ready for our trip back home to Canada. Which meant making sure everything was in order.

We had arranged for Grumpy Tequila to remain in Mexico with caretakers. Although he was an excellent traveler, he didn't do well on flights and often had to be sedated. We packed the truck with our suitcases, loaded Mia in her crate, kissed Tequila goodbye, and headed to the airport in Cabo San Lucas.

I remained conflicted on the drive; I felt strange leaving Tequila behind, I was sad to be leaving so soon, and yet excited to see our families and friends to share our Mexico experience. Plus, I knew we'd be back in the blink of an eye.

After arriving at the airport but before we could board, we had to take Mia Mukluks to the cargo hold area. Neither of us is a big fan of her flying in the cargo space. Mia Mukluks is a designated emotional support dog, but not a certified service dog, and to the airlines, there is a significant difference.

I know she will be fine, but emotionally I'm not comfortable with her being in cargo. As we walked away, I turned to look at her in her crate. Of course, my eyes started to leak. I am aware I am overreacting; dogs fly in cargo every day, yet I wish she could be in the cabin with us.

Michael grabs my hand and slightly squeezes to reassure me; he knows I worry, and off we go to find our gate.

When we board the plane, it is 28°C (86 °F) outside. The check-in attendant laughed when I tell her we're going home for Christmas. "Aren't you going the wrong way?" she asks.

"For the love of children and grandchildren," I reply, and she laughs again.

We settle in for the journey; me by the window and Michael in an aisle seat. Except for Mia Mukluks being in cargo, I love everything about flying; mostly, I love the speed at which travel is possible. Unlike Michael, who can sleep almost anywhere, I am rarely able to sleep on flights. Today was no exception, so instead, I decided to write. That's the thing about writing; you can do so anywhere.

I didn't want to forget anything about these past months, not a thing. As Michael snored softly, I wrote about all things Los Barriles. I get a little obsessed. I hold the pen so tightly I'm left with an indent in my fingers and thumb when I break from writing. It feels as though all the blood in my body leaves my extremities. My fingers and toes become icy cold. Thank goodness for fingerless gloves and toasty socks.

We had been in the air three hours already; no wonder my hand was stiff. It was time for a break, and serendipitously the refreshment cart was heading our way. I requested a hot black tea and cookies. The soothing ritual of tea is comforting and soul-filling, even when steeped and served from a paper cup.

There was a distinct chill in the cabin since we had left Cabo, likely foreshadowing what was to come. Michael woke just before we landed. He leaned over, peered out the window, and shivered, saying, "Good thing we brought our long johns."

He was right; it looked frigid; the tarmac was covered with blowing snow. Edmonton winters are cold, and from the looks of it, we were about to land in the middle of a snowstorm. Deplaning was fast, and soon we were on a mission to get Mia Mukluks. The corridors always seem endless to me upon arrival. Each corner brought another hallway, and it felt more like a maze.

As we continued the trek from the plane to Mia Mukluks, my heart began to race; I knew I would feel better once I saw her. And at last, there she was. A customs agent brought her to us. Her tail wagged so hard that it rocked the crate. Each time it hit, *thud, thud, thud, thud,* we knew she was singing to us with joy. I immediately felt better.

We had but one more small hurdle to clear: customs. I have no idea why, but customs always puts me on edge. It's not like we've done anything wrong, yet it happens every time. After answering all the usual questions, we were cleared to pass.

My daughter and youngest grandson were waiting for us to emerge from security, and when we did, there were lots of hugs and kisses for us all. Mia Mukluks lapped it all up and began doing tricks to show her joy.

Exiting the airport was shocking. It was -28°C (-18°F) with a wind-chill of -34°C (-29°F) and snowing. We went from sand and surf to snow and ice in less than six hours. It was bone-chilling. None of us were prepared for the temperature change.

Thankfully, my grandsons had bought Mia a Christmas sweater, which we immediately put under her coat as she sat in the car shivering. Mia, a Border Collie-Jack Russell-Maltese mix, only weighs eight kilograms (eighteen pounds). Her fur had just been groomed, so she, too, was freezing. Now, she was wearing a coat, sweater, and booties. She looked ridiculous.

We exited the airport, and immediately the harsh, dry wind filled our nostrils and lungs with that first breath of winter air. I have always loved the snow at Christmas, but I could pass on the cold that goes with it.

Before long, we were settled into the warm car—thank goodness for seat warmers—listening to all the latest goings-on and driving down the freeway. I had forgotten about all the neon lights and big box stores that line the freeway; so much choice—maybe too much. It was overwhelming, and yet how could it be? It had only been a few months since we left. We were both struck by the parade of neon lights and endless stores, a stark contrast in which more is better and acquisition means success.

Having left the sunny beaches only hours before wearing beachwear, and now being fully covered up from head to toe, felt strange but necessary. I could only imagine what those relocating to Canada must think upon arriving in the dead of winter.

Over the following weeks, we shared stories and celebrated Christmas. And although the temperature outside stayed frigid, our time with family was exactly as hoped for. The holiday seemed to fly by, and we knew we would soon be back in the land of sand and surf.

While in Edmonton, we talked extensively about doing more good work and about staying longer. Each time we shared the volunteer work with others, I became more passionate and felt we could do more. *But how?*

We could see there were plenty of people working to help, yet there was still so much need. During our short time in Los Barriles, we became aware of several calls for urgent more assistance and fundraising. One thing for certain was that we knew we could do more. We vowed to look deeper at how that might come about.

The Taj Mahal of Trailers

*W*e knew the Postage Stamp, albeit charming as tiny homes on wheels go, was limited. We needed something much bigger. Michael began looking for possibilities online, and there it was, the Taj Mahal of trailers. On the website page, it looked like a palace.

This fifth wheel had three slides, a spacious kitchen, a dedicated office, a big screen TV in the living room, a fireplace, a massive closet with, get this —a washer-dryer, an outdoor and indoor shower, ceiling fans, a double refrigerator, and so much more.

At about 12 meters (39 feet), it was almost double the size of the Postage Stamp. We called the RV lot, which was closing for Christmas, and told them we were very interested in seeing the trailer. We rushed down there as soon as we could.

I knew this was to be ours from the minute I sat down inside. It was a 2008 Heartland Cape Cod in mint condition. We purchased the Taj Mahal two days after Christmas, agreeing that the RV dealership would store it for us until mid-May. Oddly enough, someone had offered to buy the Postage Stamp just before we left Los Barriles for Christmas but we hadn't given it much thought.

Michael returned to Los Barriles three days later; I stayed on for another week. Something indeed had shifted—it was us. Before I knew it, my daughter, grandsons, and Mia Mukluks were at the airport and we were saying our goodbyes until summer.

Seven hours later, I was back at Number Six. I knew we'd never be the same having spent time here. We sold the Postage Stamp to two lovely people who have become fast friends, and they were so kind as to let us live in it until the end of the season. We had come to Los Barriles uncertain, and yet now, we were starting 2018 with a new purpose, entirely ready to do more.

Upon returning, we both fell into our routines. Michael was kiting when the wind whipped up and I was volunteering and working on my first international humanitarian event. The voluntourism program was called "Ignite You" and planned for February 2019. The event was designed for heart-centered souls who are doers. Participants would have a fun and life-affirming getaway while contributing to positive change.

One evening after dinner, as we sat relaxing under the stars, we reveled at how much had changed since arriving in Los Barriles. Who'd of thought this was all possible? We talked about buying the Taj Mahal in Edmonton and how it would fit at Number Six. We would need to make some adjustments to our layout since it was almost twice the size of the Stamp. I was so excited I would have a desk to work from, a washer and dryer, among other extras! We continued to banter about the past two years and what we had endured. Mostly, we affirmed how thankful we were for deciding to live this life *while we can*.

In the stillness of the night, I heard what I thought was a clapping sound on the water. It was too dark to see what all the commotion was as we sat listening. We finally gave up trying to figure it out and went to bed. But the clapping continued throughout the evening.

The following morning, I rose to the sunrise and the continuing clapping sounds. I grabbed my tea and went to investigate. Not far offshore was a fever of Mobula rays, also called Flying rays or Devil rays because their cephalic fins look like horns. We found out their mating rituals had begun and would now go on for weeks. Unlike stingrays, they don't have a stinger. These rays are huge, with wingspans that can reach up to 5 meters (17 feet). This allows them to launch themselves up to 2 meters (6 feet) in the air.

I sat and watched them in awe. Seeing them fly is magical. When they hit the water, their fins make a loud clapping sound, and it looks a lot like the ultimate belly flop. Their noisy display is to attract mates. The mating season went on for our remaining time in Los Barriles and we often fell asleep listening to their rhythmic love sounds.

Back to Canada

*O*ur remaining time in Los Barriles seemed to be accelerating. Between Michael's kiting, my work, writing, rescuing pups, and other volunteering activities, time flew by. Before we knew it, we were starting to pack up and bring an end to our season. Again, I was feeling conflicted but this time I knew why. We may have left Canada to winter in Baja, to take time to "smell the flowers," but what we discovered was our purpose. We could not wait to do more good work when we returned for the next season.

How quickly we had adapted and become attached to Los Barriles. Indeed, we found that Los Barriles becomes more of an international village without borders during the season. Year after year, people flow in and out, regrouping again with new adventures and life stories to share. We were so grateful we had become part of a global community inside an RV park.

Now, it was our turn to flow out, knowing we would be back before too long. We left with only our truck that March morning as the Postage Stamp would now forever remain in Baja. With our load lightened, we could explore the roads less traveled. On the first day, we had an uneventful drive to the Baja California Sur state border and spent the night in Guerrero Negro.

In the morning, we headed to Mexico Highway 5. This is a new highway that runs parallel to Mex 1 and is said to take about eight hours off the driving time. However, it wasn't slated to be completed until February 2020. Albeit bumpy and very rough for a 39-kilometer

(24-mile) stretch, it was worth exploring. Bumpy was a tad understated. At times, we were crawling along.

I once heard someone describe Mexico's back roads as adventurous, dangerous, and not for the faint of heart. Highway 5 was full of surprises, and unlike the warning signs in Canada and the United States, there were none on this road. Bridges just stopped without warning—and with dire consequences, if you're not paying attention.

We learned early on in Mexico the importance of looking down and self-accountability. Relying too heavily on warning signs or others was abdicating your responsibility. Highway 5 reminded us of our daily responsibility to live our best life *while we can*.

With the most challenging road behind us, the rest was beautiful. From there on, the highway is twinned, easy to drive, and borders much of the Sea of Cortez. With picturesque vistas at almost every turn, we marveled at the sea. There are many small *pueblos* along the highway.

Our destination for the night was San Felipe. Along the way, we passed Picacho Del Diablo—Devil's Peak—the highest peak on the Baja California peninsula. Rising some 3,000 meters (10,000 feet), and with boulders as large as houses, it is something that must be seen to be believed.

San Felipe is a coastal city and a beautiful gem. We arrived later in the afternoon and were moved by the beauty of this small city with a breathtaking Malecon. Located on the bay of San Felipe, it has wonderful sandy beaches and their beach camping is well-appointed and progressive. This was yet another city we would need to add to our growing list of places to spend more time in.

Today, our goal was to find a hotel, have an early dinner, and turn in early. Tomorrow, we needed to rise early to drive to the Tecate Mexican-United States border and into the United States. This meant driving Highway 5 to Mexicali and jaunting west on Highway 2. Although it would add more driving time and it was out of the way, we'd been told no drive to Baja was complete without going through wine country. Our research had indicated this was absolutely a must see and we were excited to arrive in Tecate. What we discovered that day was that wine country is the Valle de Guadalupe. Not Tecate. We would drive through wine country a year later and see breathtaking landscapes, rolling hills, and vineyards that go on for miles.

Tecate is a border city. And as borders and customs go, it is the most relaxed I have ever seen. You have probably heard of Tecate beer even if you have never been to Mexico. And when it comes to speaking Spanish, people joke about not being able to speak the language and then proudly say, *"Dos cervezas, por favor."*

Driving Baja is one of the best ways to discover the beauty and authenticity of Mexico. We crossed the border without any problems and headed for Interstate 5. Our goal was to get to Canada in two days, which would mean lots of windshield time. Our car faces were up for the challenge. We had so much to do to ready the Taj Mahal for our next epic journey.

Whirlwind

$\mathcal{S}$ummer flew by, and before we knew it, it was late October 2018, time to pack up and head to Baja. Again, we started our journey by taking the Black Ball Ferry. This time though, we were towing the Taj Mahal and at almost double the size of the Postage Stamp it was a lot more to manage. But I had faith in Michael.

Due to its size, we couldn't take the coastal highway much past Cannon Beach, but to me that is the most beautiful part of the highway. Unlike our maiden voyage with the Stamp, this trip was not about vistas and exploring; instead, this trip was about getting the Taj Mahal down to Los Barriles.

Making it through Oregon and California was fairly straightforward driving. But the Taj Mahal offered new challenges once we arrived in Mexico. Fueling up proved problematic due to its sheer height. At 4 meters (13 feet) high, we had to be more diligent with overhangs. We found few fueling stations canopies that were high enough. Michael would enter ever so gingerly; not doing so meant he could damage the top air-conditioning unit.

We stopped only to sleep and got back on the road early to maximize the daylight hours. We finally pulled into Loreto at dusk, only to discover the only available RV park was in the middle of town, and the corners were far too tight. The owner said, "no problem" and removed the wall!

As we pulled in, other RVers looked on in disbelief. I must admit I wasn't convinced this was possible. But with a couple of seasoned long-haul tractor-trailer drivers assisting, Michael felt confident. It would take thirty minutes to park correctly, but we made it, with some help from our new friends!

We arrived two days later in Los Barriles. This trip took us seven-and-a-half days.

Staking Claim

*O*ne morning, we were sitting in the Taj Mahal on the sofa, watching the sun crest the horizon. We had been back in Baja, at our beloved Site Number Six, for four weeks. Out of nowhere, Michael said, "Maybe we should buy a small *casa* with a pool."

"What?" I replied, thinking I must have heard him wrong.

"A small house with a pool," he repeated.

"I know what a *casa* is. Where on Earth is this coming from?" I asked.

At that moment, I thought he had lost his mind. Buy a property in Mexico? It seemed ludicrous and impulsive. But Michael had a good point. We would be in Los Barriles a minimum of six months per year, and if we bought a *casa*, we could also park the Taj Mahal, and have room for family and friends if they wanted to visit.

If—and it was a big if—we did this, we needed to make some changes at home. Since living the tiny home lifestyle where less is more, keeping our five-bedroom home in Canada seemed extravagant and fiscally irresponsible. It was time to downsize for sure. Maybe we could flip lifestyles? We could RV in Canada and live in a *casa* here.

Initially, it seemed far-fetched, but he was right; it was possible. We did some number crunching and discovered we could swing this if we made some changes. We would need to sell our home on Vancouver Island and downsize.

Two days later, we agreed to check some places out and see what was on the market. To our surprise, there were many homes to see in Los Barriles. We checked out one home that clicked off many must-haves for Michael. For me, it lacked the Mexican charm I wanted, and the swimming pool was too close to the front door. One wrong turn, and you would be in the deep end. The pool also leaked, and there was no covered *bodega*.

The more homes we looked at, the more issues we discovered. Not one house on the market seemed to have what we both wanted. Also, most lots would not be able to accommodate the Taj Mahal. Perhaps our expectations were too high.

We went back to the first pool house, but this time with a contractor, to see if we could do anything to solve the apparent issues. After looking things over, he said, "This house is not worth the price they are asking. If I were you, I would build a new home." That gave us something new to think about and explore.

For the next two weeks, we looked at lots, and then one day, we discovered Palo Blanco, which means white trees. Our realtor took us to a lot that ticked all the boxes. It was spacious, offered ocean views, privacy, was close to town, and only a ten-minute walk to the beach.

As we stood on the half-acre lot, we knew this was it. The lot was big enough for the Taj Mahal, and we could live in it while they built the house.

It was perfect, but could we afford it? Priced to sell and in our price range, we could hardly believe it was possible, but it was. And just like that, in December 2018, our minds shifted from thinking it seemed ludicrous to buying the lot.

At first, we questioned our logic. We'd gone from wintering in Mexico to staking a claim, putting down roots, and building a life in another country. Yet, we moved through the process at high speed, and this was only our second season in Los Barriles. We learned many things about buying land as foreigners in Mexico during those weeks.

We were on the fast track to land ownership and building in Mexico. Terms I had never heard of became part of our language.

It seemed like a lifetime ago we had talked about wintering in Los Barriles, and now we had bought a lot and were going to build a home. It was, on several occasions, overwhelming. Michael reminded me that we could do this and should—while we can. His cancer remained in remission and my aneurysms were stable. Well, as stable as aneurysms can be. In my heart, I knew he was right.

We flew home for Christmas and told our family and friends. To say it shocked them was an understatement. I think they thought us mad, and truth be told, that seemed fair.

After returning from Canada, we were more convinced than ever. If not now, when? One day over breakfast in a local café, I sketched out a home on a napkin as Michael and I talked about our wish lists.

Michael wanted an enormous *bodega* to putter in and work on the cars, and I wanted a large kitchen to bake bread and treats and make *kombucha*. We loved the idea of the house built over the *bodega*—a two-story house with two bedrooms upstairs and two hacienda style rooms (large bedrooms) with full bathrooms downstairs for rentals. We'd have an open concept with an open-air *terraza* for dining and enjoying a cup of tea while watching the sun come up. And the icing on the cake would be a rooftop *pergola*.

However, the build would have to wait until next season, and we were okay with that.

No Ordinary Afternoon

*T*wo weeks later, we were acclimatized and back to living a simpler, less complicated life. Michael was happily back to kiting.

On an otherwise ordinary afternoon, something happened to us both. I grabbed my phone to take a picture of a hummingbird preening himself in the Taj Mahal's mirrored glass picture window. I was about to post the snap on Facebook when I noticed a post about a group of Rotarians who had gone to the poorest of poor *colonias* in San Jose del Cabo. They went to make Christmas brighter for the working-class who had settled in gritty areas carved out in the harsh and unforgiving desert of shrubland.

I had never heard of these *colonias,* which are poor neighborhoods within cities or municipalities. Los Barriles is a *colonia* in the municipality of La Paz. It shocked me that a *colonia* could exist just off the beautifully manicured Mex 1 in San Jose del Cabo, tucked away, out of sight. A *colonia* of single mothers and children was scarcely seven blocks away—behind a well-stocked grocery store that caters to those with money. It is home to the poorest of the poor.

The people living here work six days a week. The daily, not hourly, wage is $7.00 per day, creating a continuous and vicious circle of poverty. Needless to say, many have limited education. This *colonia* near San Jose del Cabo is comprised mainly of abandoned, single working mothers doing their best to raise their children. It was a stark contrast to the lavish five-star resorts where many of the women worked daily; it was shocking and disheartening to discover.

The Facebook post shared the details of their plight and their immense need. As a former single mother, it was hard to read about. I vowed we'd get involved to help lift others out of such poverty. I couldn't wait to share with Michael this newfound way in which we could be of service.

On the other hand, Michael was happily kiting and unaware of what was to be a moment he would never forget. Only the day before, he mentioned how much more confident he felt when kiting. He told me, "I haven't even had a kitemare." There is a simple understanding for those who kite; kitemares are inevitable. Kiters know that there's no way to get around this; one day a kitemare will arrive and never be forgotten. But it also becomes a rite of passage to share with those who love the sport.

In true Michael fashion, he didn't ease into his first kitemare. No! His first was the most dangerous of all. All was going well when one of his lines malfunctioned and released from the kite, rendering the kite uncontrollable and useless, forcing him to do a self-rescue in high waves and strong wind gusts.

Self-rescue entails releasing the kite bar, and gathering the four lines by wrapping them around the bar, up to three-quarters of the way. He was completing his self-rescue and Michael noticed there were only three lines. Then he felt it. The fourth line was wrapping around his ankles; this was a worst-case scenario.

Miraculously, he freed his left ankle from the line, but the line remained securely wrapped around his right ankle. He kept re-wrapping the fourth line as much as possible, remaining tethered. To be tethered to your kite is one of the most dangerous situations a kiter can be in. Because if the kite powers up due to wind gust, you would be dragged through the water, face submerged, with no control of the kite and in peril of drowning. Thankfully, the kite didn't power up.

When he could finally reach the kite, he maneuvered it into the rescue sail position and turned toward shore. All the while, Michael remained dangerously tethered to the kite. He was approximately 254 meters (900 feet) offshore, in deep water. Thankfully, seeing Michael in distress, a fellow kiter took his board back to shore and shared his predicament with those onshore watching. By the time they had rallied, Michael was back on the beach. As he got out of the water, a sister kiter came to help him. As it turns out, the line had wrapped and tangled around his leg forty-five times. The woman who was helping him exclaimed, "You must have a Higher Power watching over you. You could have easily been killed today!"

When Michael returned late that afternoon, the look on his face told a story without him saying a word. He said, "I don't think I am ever going to get this." I decided this wasn't the time to share my intentions about the *colonias* with him. No, my news could wait.

It took him a day to tell me the entire story, and when he did, I tried to be neutral and supportive. Secretly, I was scared to death. It would be two weeks before he went back on the water, not because it wasn't windy, but because his confidence and resolve had taken a beating. Luckily, he got his worst kitemare out of the way early on.

In the meantime, I gathered more information on the need in these poor communities and how to be of service. One of Michael's most vital strengths is that he is a logistics kind of guy, and he focuses on the how and delivery. My most significant strength is my ability to see the big picture, leaving the details aside. We are like gasoline and fire, making for high-spirited, exciting conversations.

I was waiting until I had more details. And although not my usual style, it seemed like a smart move.

No Pillows

O ver the next few weeks, I researched the poverty gap and the most pressing needs for the poor. Was this disparity common between those who have and those who do not? Sadly, yes, the gap was real and vast. The challenge was not to oversimplify or underestimate the level of work needed to be of service.

As a big picture person, I had to put the brakes on several times to understand the culture better. I had no intention of riding in to save the day. Instead, my goal was to understand the systemic challenges and see how we could elevate, educate, and empower others. Helping at the grassroots level became my mission.

The more I leaned in, the more I learned, and I wanted to get involved. "There, but for the Grace of God, go I," played over and over in my mind. Being born in Canada afforded me this lifestyle. Sure, I worked hard and sacrificed, but my access to education, healthcare, and basic needs gave me a hand up.

In Canada, we ensure children have access to education from kindergarten through twelfth grade. Education truly is the greatest of equalizers, which further complicates issues for single mothers in Mexico. As a result, children are vulnerable and lack access to school, and the cycle repeats.

My quest to learn more led me to an orphanage in Colonia Calafia, in the municipality of La Paz, which was about an hour and a half away. The children come to the orphanage because their parents are abusive, incarcerated, or lost to addiction. It would appear my purpose was again knocking at the door. Every time I asked the Universe *what else can I do*, the answer presented itself.

Saturday, at the community market, I walked around, checking out all the vendors and visiting the puppies of Cortez Rescue. After which I got some lunch. I sought out the Sausage Lady from Germany, who makes the best barbequed Italian sausage, all smothered in deliciousness. With a little one of fewer than three months old snuggled to her, she cooks them onsite, and the aroma of grilled onions permeates the air. It is well worth the ten-minute wait.

I spotted a vendor stand for Nueva Creaçion Niñas, translated to New Creations Kids, out of the corner of my eye. This was the orphanage I had heard so much about. Their table contained wooden pens, wind chimes, notebooks, frames, and more. The wares are made entirely by the orphanage's children and created out of donated supplies and equipment.

I spoke with the two volunteers managing the booth. They shared with me the plight of the children who passed through the orphanage's doors. It was heartbreaking; some children had been there for years. Abandoned and forgotten, these children ended up at the orphanage. One gentleman invited me to come to the Annual Art Festival the next day to meet the children and the caregivers.

Over dinner, I told Michael about my adventures but held off telling him about my crazy, almost ridiculous idea. I wasn't ready to voice it yet. It was safe and stewing nicely in my head and heart. However, I did tell him I wanted us to go to the Art Festival.

My vision was to build a platform with a team of people coming together to help the *colonias*, Cortez Rescue, SNAP, New Creations Kids orphanage and to assist in situations where there was immediate and deep need. Our purpose would be to serve others and provide a hand-up from a grassroots level. We would work with locals and help to educate, elevate, and empower others. My crazy, big idea was founding a not-for-profit society. It was a lofty plan and full of challenges, but it was also promising and could contribute to change.

The name came to me almost immediately one morning as I sat drafting out my initial goals:

TEAM HUMANITY BAJA
Heart and Souls of Change.

The following day, I was both excited and nervous. I already felt attached to the children, yet I hadn't even met them. We arrived at the Art Festival early. My sole intention was to learn more about the orphanage and to meet the caregivers and children of New Creations Kids.

We initially met foster parents Roberto and Alma. Within seconds, the children swarmed Michael, Mia Mukluks, and me. Each child wanted to pet Mia Mukluks and sit with us. Before I knew it, three of the youngest girls were sitting on my lap as I sat on the grass. Their laughter and glee enveloped me, and Mia Mukluks was lapping up all the attention.

And then, the youngest of the children stood up and looked directly at me. She was staring intently at my sunglasses. I thought she was going to reach over to take them off my face, but no. What she did instead cemented my involvement with the orphanage. Samantha leaned in to me, touched my cheek, and then kissed me.

The tears welled up while I told myself, *No, you cannot cry in front of these kids.* I stood quickly and explained I'd be right back, using a trip to the *bano* as my excuse. This little one was so tiny. She was not even two years old. One of the adults told me, "You look like her mother," and with that, I could no longer hold in my emotions. I had to take a walk and let my tears fall out.

Ten minutes later, a bit more composed, I came back. We stayed with the children until the market was fully buzzing and they returned to their table to sell their wares. After meeting the children and adults that day, I was convinced the crazy, ambitious idea I had been concocting could work.

I knew we needed to do a site visit to the orphanage and gather donations for the *colonias*. We arranged for the site visit the following week. I'm not sure what I expected. I had never been to an orphanage before, and I had no frame of reference. Be that as it may, I was sure the conditions would not meet standards in Canada or the United States.

When we arrived, I was pleased to see the children were clean and fed, but they lacked so many necessities. On this day, none wore shoes because they kept their shoes for school. I could tell they were doing their very best to care for the children, but funding was limited. They nearly always ran out of money before they ran out of the month.

One of the scenes that struck me hard was their play area. It had a patch of sand and a few pieces of broken outdoor equipment. Off to the left was the workshop building where the wares they sold to raise money were made. Immediately, I noticed there was not a single piece of safety equipment, yet the children used heavy-duty machines on a daily basis. The youngest at work was only seven. The thought of a child suffering an accident because there were no safety glasses or gloves made me shudder.

Next, we toured the dorms, which may have made me the saddest of all. In a two-story cinderblock house, the boys and girls are separated by a floor. A caretaker slept in the boy's dorm at night. Imagine being a young child, waking up at night from a bad dream, with no one to comfort you, having been taken away from your parents. Each bed was perfectly made, but something was lacking. There was not a single pillow. I thought of those little ones laying their heads down every night. Something so basic as a pillow was a luxury.

The bathrooms were in desperate need of repair, and there wasn't hot water for the showers. Later, we learned water was delivered to the orphanage, and it wasn't uncommon for the tank to run out before the month's end. Two of the doors to the bathrooms hung perilously to a frame held by wire; the need was real.

There was no personalization in the boys' section, with only minor touches added in the girls' dorm. A memory flooded my mind of my own children's rooms. Each had personalized their rooms with so many little pieces of their lives. A childhood room is part of growing up, claiming your space, and developing your individual identity, yet, here, there were no signs, drawings, posters, or anything with their names for these children.

I felt sad and a bit overwhelmed. These children had already lost so much. After touring the facility, we sat outside to enjoy the sunshine; the girls loved my phone and taking pictures. Being together and watching them interact with us so naturally, I realized how children are shaped to become resilient; all they seem to ask for is love and attention.

They invited us to play volleyball with a vinyl ball over a rope net. Since our Spanish skills were still lacking, we used hand motions and played a game. We decided Michael would be on the girl's team, and I would be with the boys. We didn't care about the points or keeping score; it was all about the time shared. After a while, we were all laughing so hard no one could even hit the ball.

In the end, we decided the team I was on had won. Not that it mattered, but there was celebrating and dancing. For a few minutes, I forgot about what was lacking. All that mattered was the laughter. After the game, we bought pizza and pop to celebrate, and the kids devoured every bite.

We left the orphanage better humans than when we arrived. These children had served us much more than they knew. I have a few treasured photos from that day, but the emotional impact will be forever imprinted on my heart.

The idea of Team Humanity Baja was morphing every day. Soon, it became much bigger than I could have imagined and it was far more ambitious than anything I had ever done before. Seeing the need firsthand further pushed my desire to do whatever I could. It's impossible to unsee extreme poverty and, worse, the longing for love in their eyes, and do nothing.

The non-profit organization was taking shape, and also becoming all-consuming. We would become an umbrella, grassroots society focusing on four distinct groups: *colonias*, the Cortez Rescue, SNAP, and—yes—the New Creation Kids orphanage.

I continued my research; I needed a solid and viable plan. It still wasn't time to share my goal with anyone yet, even—and perhaps especially—Michael, as this plan would directly affect him. Now, having a better understanding of the need (which I knew only scratched the surface and was a symptom of something much bigger), a plan emerged of how Team Humanity Baja could help lift others.

Finally, it was almost time to share with Michael. I met three key stakeholders who had critical information about the orphanage and the *colonias*. I discovered gaps in service delivery, and they, too, were stretched thin and shared concerns. Team Humanity Baja could fill those gaps.

Helen Keller said it best. "Alone we can do so little, together we can do much." We didn't have to do all things, only help bridge the gaps and perhaps fill some gaping holes. The more I learned how things worked, the more our service role became clearer.

Service before Self

A week or so after visiting the orphanage, I met with two women who I knew were community-oriented and dedicated to helping those in need: Celeste Gut and Pamela Conzton.

Celeste, a retired nurse full of compassion and empathy with boundless energy, shared the practical and desperate need of the *colonias* and the orphanage. She presented her experience with an unbiased and factual account that was chilling and truthful. She spoke of the health challenges, immediate and daily needs, and the long-term impact of poverty.

Pamela, also retired, is driven to serve. She shared from a place of deep heartache. Her eyes filled with tears—when speaking of the hunger and no running water. Pamela shared what she had witnessed, a level of poverty no one should ever endure. She juxtaposed these hidden, squalid areas with the manicured main streets prepared for those who visit Mexico, and described the distressing living conditions of those who work in the fancy tourist resorts.

These two women had seen firsthand the devastation of the *colonias*, especially the one in Esperanza, and had visited the orphanage. They also saw gaps and missing pieces that only a grassroots movement could likely provide. What Celeste and Pamela had witnessed was life-altering. We all have our reasons for volunteering and giving back. For some, working behind the scenes in small but steady ways feels right; for others, it's something bigger and bolder. One thing is for sure, whatever the reason for giving back, it's perfect.

As we sat in Maria's Café, having lunch and talking, we were convinced Team Humanity was needed. No matter how big or small our efforts, we knew we could make a difference. It was important to keep our purpose focused on elevating, educating, and empowering people, all while respecting the culture.

As we planned our first trip to the *colonias*, our excitement grew. We were clear on our mission: we were a grassroots movement meant to serve and help fill the gaps, and to do whatever it took to bring positive and lasting change. We believed every act made a difference. We had no idea what would happen, but we were all up for it.

I was so honored when they agreed to become members of Team Humanity Baja. Truth be told, none of us knew what we were about to undertake. But these two kindred souls said yes despite there being no formal plan. We only had our heartfelt desires to help and to be of service to others. I left the café energized—and also a bit terrified. *Who was I to think we could make the type of impact we desired?*

Then, I remembered a saying I had heard once and instantly loved: "If you're not part of the solution, you're part of the problem."

So, no matter Team Humanity Baja's size, the three of us were clear that we were called to do what we could. Of course, I wanted Michael to be a part of Team Humanity. I knew he would also love the idea of working on projects together and helping others. Big picture thinking only works in conjunction with sound operational delivery, and it was time to unleash the big idea.

That night over dinner, I shared my idea. It poured out of me at lightning speed. Team Humanity Baja was no longer just a bunch of thoughts coming together in my noggin. I was so excited my hands were shaking, I tried to pace myself, but my enthusiasm took over. And when I had finished, I was out of breath. Michael's first question was, "What can we do to help?"

Though his response caught me off guard, I was elated. I was prepared for logistics questions. It was as though he had known I'd been cooking something up all along. I also thought he would be worried about my health and not taking enough time to recharge. I had anticipated all of that, not this. I was ready to share all my reasons why it was a must-do—at least for me. I was all ready to explain how I needed a purpose; I needed to give back in a meaningful way.

But none of that explaining or justification was necessary. Instead, I switched gears and jumped right into laying out my initial plan to do a donation run in three weeks to the *colonias*. I told Michael I wasn't sure how much we could raise, but we could at least contribute something. Secretly, I was hoping for three fully-loaded trucks of food and goods. I may not be good at reining myself in but I am great at big picture dreaming and thinking.

We may have initially come to winter and relax in Mexico, but this was much bigger and exciting.

The Cancha

*R*ight on cue, three weeks later, the day finally arrived, and not a minute too soon. We met at 7:30 that morning and loaded the trucks. My heart beat faster as each truck pulled onto the highway ready to make their deliveries. We were headed to San Jose del Cabo to the *colonia* of Esperanza.

We were a makeshift, ragtag, group of committed people with six overflowing trucks and eight eager and excited volunteers—a convoy of goodness. It was truly a sight to see. We had collected bandages, bedding, books, toys for the children, clothing, food, hygiene products, pencils and paper, pots and pans, first aid equipment, and much more.

As we drove behind Alma Cota, our guide, I was over the moon, excited, grateful, and filled with anticipation. Celeste, Pamela, and I had sat in Maria's Café barely a month earlier saying yes without knowing how we could pull anything like this off.

The day was another beautiful day in Mexico; sunny and warm. We were to meet at Sorina's grocery store just off the beautifully-manicured highway, lined with bougainvillea of all colors. Alma would lead us into the *colonia* and to the *cancha*. In Mexico, every community has a *cancha*, an area that serves as a meeting place. In most *colonias*, they are paved and resemble a basketball court.

Colonias are simply towns of larger municipalities. Specific *colonias* are typically built on government land and over time, some of the land can be owned by the residents. Squatters are typical, with little to no means to establish themselves. The inequalities of the working class that often take jobs in the resorts are glaring. We drove into the community on a barely impassable road, situated only seven blocks off the highway. The contrast is shocking and impossible not to see. The abject poverty is like a punch in the gut. And yet, only blocks away, you'll find an idyllic portrait of Mexico.

In this *colonia*, a place many called home, stood shanty shacks with tarps for roofs; there was no plumbing, minimal access to water, and dangerously-erected and improvised electrical poles and power lines. These shanties could never provide protection in a hurricane; it was heartbreaking. The farther we drove in, the more crushing conditions we saw. Electrical wires dangerously dangling amid dirt-floor homes constructed of scrap building materials, rusted, corrugated metal roofs, cardboard tacked up over windows, and what I guess you could call foundations propped up with pieces of wood, cinder blocks, and even sticks.

Most who live in these impoverished areas earn less than eight dollars or around 164 pesos a day.

When we finally arrived to the meeting area, we were all a little overwhelmed. For many of us, this was our first time entering deep into such a place. People were waiting for us, with at least a dozen dogs wandering about, ranging from large to small, and most were noticeably underweight.

We parked, and climbed out of the trucks. We were about to head into the *cancha* when two large dogs got into a vicious scrap. Fur was flying, and the gnashing of teeth was frightening. Thank goodness, Michael and another local woman took charge of the situation and were able to separate them as the rest of us stood frozen. We all cheered for the day's heroes when the dogs limped away, likely more from bruised egos than serious injury.

Alma then introduced me to the matriarch of the *colonia*, Carmen, a petite but commanding woman of vintage, her hair pulled gracefully to one side. Her eyes were framed with wisdom lines, telling the story of a woman who had worked hard all her life. She wore a simple skirt and chiffon blouse. Carmen's smile was warm and inviting. Her hands were weathered and wrinkled yet gentle and soft when she took my hand in hers. With Alma translating, I thanked Carmen for allowing us to serve in our small way.

Then we got down to business setting up to distribute donations. Unlike the others I had seen, I noticed that this *cancha* was a rickety structure, consisting of four poles in the dirt with some corrugated metal tied to the poles to keep it in place. Almost everyone we met was barefoot; this troubled me, given the trash and dog feces. Again, we learned that shoes are saved for work and school days; this was neither.

When we first arrived, there were about twenty people, but within ten minutes, there were more than 200 gathered. We had lots of donations, but I feared we would run out. People kept coming and coming. At one point, the sheer volume of people had pushed us into the makeshift tire wall on the backside of the *cancha*.

Soon, all the donations had been distributed except for one brown vinyl suitcase of men's clothing. A young man, Javier, who had been standing off to the side, tentatively approached us and asked if he could look through the case. He told us he had an interview the next day. He smoothed out the creases with his hands as he tried some of the clothes on. This smoothing of the wrinkles did not escape any of us. Tears began to well again.

We noticed his shoes were being held together with duct tape. He saw us looking at them and told Alma he had walked from his small village to Cabo in hopes of finding work, and in doing so, his shoes were beyond repair.

Michael spoke up. *"Javier, lo siento."*

As luck would have it, some lovely dress shoes and black socks were in the suitcase and went nicely with the other clothes. Now, Javier had everything he needed, and his eyes sparkled.

"Muchas gracias, Dios te bendiga," Javier said, as he took my hands. This, I understood. "Thank you so much, God bless you."

"De nada," I replied, trying to push back the tears. *"Dios te bendiga, Javier."*

Another man, Francisco, who declared himself a security guard for the women, approached us after all the women and children were gone to ask if we had any food left. In the back of our truck, a bag of rice had fallen out. He was so ecstatic, he too, was looking for a job and had not eaten in two days. Every single person moved me that day—every single person. I am not sure what I expected to see. What I did see was compassion, kindness, and sharing. I saw women with their children, and in them, I saw myself.

We asked for permission to take photos because we wanted to share their need to encourage more donations in the future. A mother asked me to take a picture of her with her young son. It was a mother-to-mother moment; as she held him up, their faces beamed with big smiles.

Carmen told Alma that one young woman, Juanita, had only arrived yesterday as we were handing out donations. She had arrived with little more than a suitcase for her and her daughter. Currently, Juanita was staying with someone until she could get a job and find safe housing.

Safe housing in the poor *colonias* is an oxymoron. But those who are here care for one another. To enter these communities with donations, you must have a guide, and there are protocols to follow for safety and security. We never once felt threatened or unsafe; on the contrary. Nor did I want anyone to feel unsafe.

As Juanita walked down the line gathering donations, she took very little. Seemingly uncomfortable and embarrassed, I thanked her for allowing us to serve as she passed, and we each encouraged her to take more.

"*Mas, Juanita, mas,*" we urged.

"*No gracias, Señora,*" Juanita graciously declined.

We knew Juanita needed so much more. As she carried her daughter on her hip, she selected a set of twin sheets, two towels, and two pairs of flip-flops.

Every moment we were there was impactful. Our lives and perceptions would never be the same. We learned so much that day about who we are, what we believe, and our role in lifting others. And there were tears, lots of them, gratitude, and humility.

I tried my best not to cry, but I failed as I watched mother after mother stocking their baskets. I witnessed grace like never before. I felt embarrassed by the lack of knowledge of the need that was just off the manicured highway. When everything was gone and people had left, making their way back to their makeshift homes, it felt as though we had much work to do. And yet, we felt hopeful; at least we had begun.

We thanked Carmen and told her we would return in the fall. We took a picture and hugged each other for the moment we had shared.

And then, as we exited the *colonia*, we drove by Juanita, carrying the flip flops, with the sheets and towels dangling just above the ground, as she walked hand-in-hand with her daughter. My heart ached for her. I remember the struggles of being a single mom. It was hard, but nothing like this.

I wanted to stop the truck to tell her, *you're not alone. I see you, we all do, and we'll be back.* But we didn't stop. Not because I didn't want to, but because I had no way to convey the words. At that moment, Juanita had no way of knowing her impact on me.

She looked away as we passed by; we had done so little to ease her struggle. As she walked on, I could not help but think of the refugees that come to Canada. Except she was not a refugee, this was her country, and life had been unkind.

Regrouping after our first run as Team Humanity Baja, all I could think of was that we would do better next time. Our goal was to encourage and ease the struggle, and for some, we did, but Juanita and her wee daughter weighed heavy on my heart.

In addition to those who had committed and joined us that day, a dear friend visiting from Canada was never the same. She and her husband had not expected to see the level of poverty they witnessed. Dianna returned to Canada and committed to being the change. She shared our work and mission with anyone who would listen. Her biggest desire was to return every year to serve. Sadly, we lost Dianna a year later. Until she passed, she spread the word about the plight of those in need.

"Service before self" became my daily mantra. There was so much to do, and we were just learning about the culture and protocols. What we realized that day is we would need to get a cargo trailer when we were back in Canada. When I shared our mission to serve the *colinas* on Facebook, friends and acquaintances near and far asked how they, too, could help; it was truly heartwarming. A cargo trailer would be added to our wish list for Team Humanity Baja.

Big Changes

*A*fter the second winter in Los Barriles ended in the early spring of 2019, we packed up once again to return to Vancouver. We would arrive in time to cheer on our grandson, a competitive goalkeeper, who was playing in a regional soccer tournament. I refer to these moments as privileged Grandma duties. The timing was perfect as we had much to do, one of which was selling our home.

I was excited and yet torn. Once we sold our house, we would be without a home in our own country. On the now familiar route north, we planned to make a few stops on our must-see list that we had been compiling. We discussed a variety of options and decided the first stop would be El Requesón in Bahia Concepción.

We turned into the *playa* there and lumbered down the bumpy, sandy road with the Taj Mahal in tow. This beach became our all-time favorite and is frequented by locals and tourists but this early in the spring, there were few others on the beach. We were lucky to have arrived at low tide which allowed us to cross the sand spit and explore. After which we had a beach fire and roasted Italian bratwurst. Although it was too cool to paddleboard, it was magical to be glamping right on the beach boondocking-style.

The following morning, we took a stroll on the beach just before sunrise. I captured a picture of the truck and Taj Mahal as the sun was cresting the horizon. It was the perfect depiction of living a nomadic lifestyle.

Getting first to Vancouver for the tournament and then back to Vancouver Island as quickly as possible seemed important given all we had to do. We were not only selling our house but we were also moving our primary address from British Columbia to Alberta. It all seemed over the top, but I reminded myself this was the time to do this *while we still could.*

After a busy summer, by August, we'd packed what belongings we could fit into a moving truck that would be held in storage in San Diego before heading onto Los Barriles. We hauled a cargo trailer of 5,443 kilograms (12,000 pounds) of donations, which we aptly named Kindness, to San Diego for pick up in early 2020.

In September, we pulled out of the driveway for the last time with the Taj Mahal in tow. It was a bittersweet moment. I loved the Island; we were leaving behind family and friends; it was hard, but it was now or never. I thought about all the choices we had faced since 2015, and where we were today.

Life choices are hard. As I used to say to my children, "there is a reaction to every action." Unlike the first time we made this epic drive—when Michael and I had way more questions than answers—we had "gone and done it!" We were officially homeless in Canada. It wasn't like we were giving up our citizenship, but now our ties were only family and friends. It was freeing but terrifying.

We decided to bring my SUV down to Los Barriles, which meant I would drive solo. I had never driven for more than seven hours before, and certainly not for days. Several friends had offered to drive, but I wanted to say I drove to Mexico; it was important.

I followed Michael as he towed the Taj Mahal. This gave us an extra set of eyes from behind. The total length of the truck plus the fifth wheel was more than 17 meters (57 feet). It was something to see on the windy roads. I could only imagine what lay ahead. I decided it was best not to focus on the perils of Mex 1 until I had to.

We devised a plan to communicate using walkie-talkies. These were only to be used in emergencies, separations, or when it was time to announce a much-needed break. This worked well most of the time. Since I could check for clearances and see if anything looked off from behind, Michael could let me know of impending road hazards.

Here we were, another moment of "while I still can." I never imagined myself driving 4,400 kilometers (2,734 miles) alone. This trip was not about vistas and scenery but safety and efficiency. Being in the driver's seat gave me far more respect for Michael's talents. The I-5 interstate could easily accommodate the Taj Mahal through the States, but once we got into Mexico, there were many scary moments.

But we made it, and I was never so glad to see the Taj Mahal parked after we arrived.

Casa de Cielo

*B*ack in March 2019, we met with several builders in Mexico and selected one we felt had impeccable credentials and experience before returning to Canada. We agreed to start building our new home in January 2020.

We named it Casa de Cielo; a home of peace and tranquility. *Cielo* has many meanings, including sky, heaven, sweetheart, and darling. For us, the translation is House in the Sky. Standing nearly 9 meters tall (29 feet), Casa de Cielo would feel close to the sky. At night we would be enveloped by the stars.

Our design was to have a simple, open concept home with Mexican influence with a few modern touches. There would be large sliding doors and a spacious outdoor terrace for dining and taking in the glorious sunrise; rich, brown-stained concrete floors throughout, tinted concrete counters, varnished *parota* wood cabinetry and doors, and indigo blue tile accents.

All this in two stories with complete roof access and 360-degree breathtaking views of the ocean and mountains. There would be two bedrooms upstairs, two primary suites on the main floor, and an outdoor kitchen. The property vision was to create a desert oasis with bougainvillea, roselle hibiscus (in Mexico known as *Jamacia*), cactus, palms, lavender, endemic trees, and more.

We broke ground on schedule in January 2020. We wanted to live onsite during the build, so we relocated the Taj Mahal to Number Seventeen, Palo Blanco. It was exciting and terrifying at the same time.

Soon, our site was abuzz with workers, cement trucks, and services. They started at 8:00 a.m. and worked until 5:00 p.m., Monday through Friday. On Saturdays, they kept at it from 9:00 a.m. until 1:00 p.m. Often, I shuddered as I watched the workers carry huge buckets of mixed cement up the ladders on their shoulders with no safety equipment. These men worked incredibly hard, and the building went up fast.

Then, it all stopped on April 6, 2020. In fact, the world came to an abrupt halt as we all navigated the Covid-19 pandemic. Over the next two plus years, the house construction limped along. What was to take five months took twenty-eight months, and two contractors. Sadly, the first contractor abandoned the build when he found new jobs. We were left with a home seventy-five percent complete and scrambling to find a new, reputable contractor.

At times, we questioned our decision to build in Mexico. We knew that construction was different in Mexico, but we didn't expect our first contractor to abandon our project. As with all such undertakings, diligence, patience, and stick-to-itiveness are necessary. We thought we had selected the right person, but we had not. We learned some things the hard way, but we stuck it out. There were some tough days, for sure.

We lived in the Taj Mahal for more than two years. We learned a lot about ourselves during that time, about compromise, and tiny home living. I'm forever grateful we were called to Baja to serve and live our legacy.

Mexico taught us how blessed we were, that less truly is more, happiness is a choice, and life is ours to live. Mexico taught us to treasure every relationship and live with gratitude and humility in all we do.

Sunset

*T*oday, sitting peacefully on the terrace at Casa de Cielo, I sip my high-test tea, watching the magnificent sunset, and listening to the doves and songbirds sing. With the scent of lavender and budding trees filling the air, I find myself in awe. I can't imagine what life would have looked like had we not decided to live *while we can*.

We have come so far and learned so much. We are now permanent residents of Mexico and maintain our Canadian citizenship. Enjoying Mexico in the cooler months and Canada in the summer months is such a blessing. Today, we are even more involved in our beloved Los Barriles. My Spanish continues to improve and my heart continues to grow. We may have had bumps, but we have no regrets.

Life is fatal; you have two choices: be a spectator or an active participant. You, me, we; are all going to pass someday, but not today, so don't stop living today.

I will not go to my funeral twice; I will live fully *while I can*. We are more than the circumstances, and I'll be damned if I live waiting to die.

When I was young, my youth was squandered and less appreciated. I did not know what I know now. At six, my view of life was limited and yet I vowed to live to be one hundred and six. Why? Because I wanted to celebrate Canada's next birthday and enjoy a piece of birthday cake.

At twenty-nine, I lost a kidney to cancer and lived. At fifty-five, I gained clarity about the fragility of life. Today, I realize I have fewer days ahead and more behind me. It is why I am living my best life, w*hile I can*.

My wish is for you to do the same.

Be present today, find your purpose, and live your legacy *while you can*.

For some, this might mean epic road trips, working abroad, taking exotic vacations, or living the uncomplicated, simple life and enjoying *every* moment!

Ultimately, we can either let the cards we have been dealt define our life or we can live a defining life. It's our choice.

And yes, I still have that napkin with the first drawing of our *casa*, now framed and hanging for me to see as a reminder that dreams do come true.

*La vida es una aventura
que tenemos el privilegio de disfrutar.*

Life is an adventure
we are privileged to enjoy.

Then, They Said YES!

*M*ark Twain had it right when he wrote, "charitable views of men and things cannot be acquired by vegetating in one little corner of the earth all one's lifetime."

The first step in forming Team Humanity Baja required formalizing it as a not-for-profit society. This legality would have to be completed in Canada. Little did I know then it would take two years and a lot of paperwork. Meanwhile, our team has done some fantastic things.

Recently, I overheard Celeste Gut sharing why she said, "Yes!" back on the day we met for lunch with Pamela Conzton at Maria's Café.

"We were three women who had the joy and privilege of spending a great deal of time in Los Barriles, Baja California Sur. Each of us was volunteering for various causes during the fall of 2018. We just wanted to help. None of us had a desire to change the world. Our aim is to aid the people here in whatever way we can to ease the daily battle to survive.

"Our causes have included support for Nueva Creaçion Niñas in La Paz. This is a home for the children who have been left behind, mostly due to addiction. We have helped Cortez Rescue, which cares for and finds forever homes for abandoned and surrendered dogs. The SNAP initiative (Spay, Neuter, Awareness, Prevention) is also under our fundraising efforts to prevent the overpopulation and abandonment of cats and dogs. We take aid to the poorest of poor in local *colonias* where women and children live in extreme poverty.

"It began with three committed women, and now Jo has founded our society. We remain a grassroots organization that is adaptable and fluid. I am honored to have been asked to serve and am grateful to continue to support Team Humanity Baja."

The following fall, I asked Pamela why she said yes, and she shared her thoughts with me.

"Once Jim, my husband, and I visited the colony of mostly single mothers and children in Colonia Esperanza to bring food, a meal, household items, clothes, and shoes to those living on the outskirts of San Jose Del Cabo in Baja California Sur, Mexico, I knew we had to do more. These women are the poorest of the poor, struggling daily to survive. There was no running water that day, and the magnitude of poverty hit us both. Even though we were only temporarily easing their struggle, their gratitude touched us.

"Returning to Los Barriles with the small group of Rotarians that day, I knew there had to be a way. Serendipitously, Jo invited me to lunch and asked if I was interested in becoming a founding member of Team Humanity Baja, an idea she was only just formulating. We all wanted to do more, but we could do even more together.

"We got right down to business; the need was ongoing and urgent. Together, we were planning our next trip, assigning tasks, and setting dates. There was no shortage of work or enthusiasm. The donations came in faster than we could process them.

"We needed food, household goods, clothing, shoes, and bedding, and we received that and more. Our mission was to serve the most vulnerable in the community; Team Humanity Baja would become an umbrella organization to cover the local colonies, an orphanage in La Paz, Spay, Neuter Awareness Prevention clinics, and Cortez Rescue. Our first trip back to the *colonia* was more of a convoy. It was a massive success.

"I am blessed and honored to be part of this grassroots not-for-profit."

None of this would have been possible without our board members. Please join me in acknowledging these committed, compassionate, knowledgeable, generous humans who said "Yes!" without hesitation.

Along with our members-at-large, these are all dedicated people, each with expertise that compliments the other. More so, they are action takers and doers. Together, we are continuously looking at those we serve and searching for ways to bring more, to elevate, educate, and empower.

Board members Brenda Hammon and William Portwood reside in Alberta, Canada. Both have extensive financial backgrounds and have been instrumental in raising funds. I asked why they said, "Yes!" and here is what they wrote:

"Because we knew that any monies that we collected and donated to the organization went to those in need; not for administration fees but right to the root of the problem. We both know Jo and Michael. They are the boots on the ground in the area that requires the most help.

"Helping and serving others has always been a part of who we are; having someone in place where the money goes directly to where it is needed is imperative. We have both witnessed firsthand the work Team Humanity Baja does. Having worked alongside Jo and Michael, we were able to see firsthand where the money goes."

Rachel Dyer resides in British Columbia. She recently shared her experience as a board member:

"Whilst I knew that it would be something very special, I never knew exactly how special being part of Team Humanity Baja would be. Initially, my role entailed sorting and packing donations and we had thousands of pounds to sort through in Canada. Those donations were transported to Mexico. I knew that the donations were important, but I have to tell you: I was completely overwhelmed with the amount of donations that came in.

"I have been lucky enough to experience some of what Team Humanity Baja does firsthand and I have been touched to my core. In 2020, just before the pandemic, I flew down to Mexico to take part in the "Ignite You" event held in Baja. One of our first stops was to the New Creations Kids Orphanage in La Paz. To see the joy in the kids' faces when we arrived was unforgettable. They were so excited that we were there.

"We were able to help teach them how to make things so that they can sell them at the local markets. Donations are fantastic but it's also so important to help teach the children how to be self-sufficient, how to earn their own money, and how to become independent.

"I had the pleasure of doing hand-painting with some of the younger ones and they were so keen to learn English words and to teach me some Mexican words. One little girl totally stole my heart. As we were leaving, she came up to me and gave me a big kiss on my cheek. That, for me, was why I was there. That was why I need to be a part of this.

"Our next stop was Cortez Rescue. Oh, the puppies, so many puppies! It was heartbreaking to see so many dogs needing homes. I flew down with a suitcase of dog collars and leashes to donate. I soon realized although every donation is important, what I had brought with me was just not enough. To know that so many of these animals were left to live on the streets, struggling to find food, but now have a chance, thanks to this rescue mission and the donations.

"I feel as if these words are not enough to explain how important Team Humanity Baja is. It's so much more than can ever be put into words. This entire experience changed me and changed how I look at so many things. It has made me even more grateful for what I have. That's why I did not hesitate to say "Yes!" when I was asked to join the board. I have seen firsthand how important Team Humanity Baja and it is an honor to be a part of it."

Last, but certainly not least, is Michael Dibblee. Needless to say, he is the glue that keeps everything together. Always supportive, never complaining, he says "Yes!" with his big heart and smile, long before I ever need to ask. For Michael, it's simple: we have so much we must give back.

elle

Team Humanity Baja

Thank you for reading *While I Can*. I hope you are inspired to live your life *while you can*. What's next? Team Humanity Baja carries on our work for the causes I've described and others as the need arises. Our goal, with your support, is to ease the life of others. To empower, educate, and elevate. It's a massive undertaking, but together I know we can assist in being the change.

Please help us raise more funds. *While I Can* will donate to Team Humanity Baja with every book purchase.

Are you interested in joining Team Humanity Baja? We would love to have your help. A few ways to support us are by:

» Sharing this book with co-workers, family, and friends.

» Adding positive reviews on Amazon. This is truly helpful! Your review and recommendation will significantly impact our ability to raise more funds for the Team Humanity Baja legacy fund.

» Following us on Facebook and Instagram:
facebook.com/groups/teamhumanitybaja
instagram.com/jo_dibbleeauthor_

» Tagging us with #teamhumanitybaja when you share your reviews on Facebook or Instagram.

» Joining us in person at upcoming Team Humanity Baja activities.

We would be forever grateful for your continued support and sharing of Team Humanity Baja. Please stay tuned for updates and for more enduring stories of change at jodibblee.com.

Acknowledgements

Few authors can write and produce great works on their own. As a person with dyslexia, I would be lost without my team of loving, talented friends and professionals who are steadfastly dedicated to helping me create the best work I can. Although my initial diagnosis of Vascular Ehlers-Danlos and the three aneurysms almost derailed me, it didn't. I am grateful; as it turns out, a normal life gives one little to write about.

My heartfelt thanks to...

> » Kim Duke, for your dedication and directions to write it all down, and for creating a safe space to share what matters most. You challenged me to go deeper and cheered me on when I was stuck.
>
> » Celeste Benedict-Gut, for your inspiration in moments of doubt. Your proofreading and feedback helped me see my words through a reader's eyes.
>
> » Jain Lemos, for your editing experience, research, and talent. Your commitment to *While I Can* has been unwavering.
>
> » Josh Aldrich, for your expertise and website development.
>
> » Julie Shipman, photographer, for your generous donation of images and restoration of photos for the book.
>
> » Rosario M. Soley, for your vision and talent in capturing the spirit of the book though your illustrations; you so get me.

My loves, thank you for your love and support, especially to...

> » my children and grandchildren, for inspiring me to keep going and living.
>
> » my husband Michael, for sharing this journey with me. What a ride we continue to have.
>
> » my friends, for standing with me and cheering me on.

About the Author

*J*o Dibblee is foremost a humanitarian. As an international bestselling and award-winning author and speaker, her work has been featured multiple times in Canadian media and the *Huffington Post*. She is the founder and CEO of Frock Off, Inc.

Her previous book, *Bella's Dash: How Our Pup Rescued Us*, is a collection of heartwarming stories and information on the impact of dogs in healing. Co-authored by her husband, Michael Dibblee, *Bella's Dash* is a powerful account of the toll and plight of first responders. Michael, a retired firefighter, served as a first responder, professional firefighter, and Dive Rescue Specialist for thirty years.

Jo's first book, *Frock Off: Living Undisguised*, is a tell-all, true crime book. Jo spent thirty-five years in hiding as a key witness in a murder investigation. She is also the author of *From Best Kept Secret to Success in Life, Love & Business*, where Jo shares the common elements we each face in the human experience of moving from best kept secret to success.

Her latest book, *While I Can: Finding Purpose and Legacy in a Distant Land*, is about daring to live courageously no matter what cards you have been dealt. Jo tells the story of how a retired firefighter and his wife throw caution to the wind and follow their hearts. Amid health challenges and devastating diagnoses, they trade the comfort of their spacious home on beautiful Vancouver Island for a tiny home on wheels to find meaning and new passion in Baja California Sur, Mexico.

www.ingramcontent.com/pod-product-compliance
Lightning Source LLC
Chambersburg PA
CBHW051423090426
42737CB00014B/2806